Endorsements

"In the compass of this small volume, Douglas Bond somehow manages to corral all the mysterious paradoxes of John Knox: the thunderous pulpit and the closet intercessions, the soaring intellect and the humble home life, the boldness and the meekness, the might and the weakness. In other words, Bond has captured the very essence of this remarkable model for reformational ministry."

—Dr. George Grant
Pastor, East Parish Presbyterian Church
Franklin, Tennessee

"I am delighted to recommend Douglas Bond's latest book, *The Mighty Weakness of John Knox*. Bond has written many, mainly children's, books on sixteenth- and seventeenth-century Scottish church history. He writes with the passion of a man who believes that the church today needs, for its spiritual good and sanity, to learn about the church of yesterday. In choosing to write a book on John Knox, Bond has done the church today a great service. Knox was the towering figure of the Scottish Reformation. In many ways, he was a reluctant hero, conscious as he was of his own weaknesses. However, as the title of the book makes plain, Knox's sense of weakness was overwhelmed by his sense of God's greatness. Indeed, as Bond shows us throughout his book, it was Knox's constant sense of his own weakness that enabled the Lord to use him so mightily in His service. When Knox was asked to account for the wonderful success of the Scottish Reformation, he replied, 'God gave his Holy Spirit in great abundance to simple men.' Read this book. Learn from this book. Thank God for men like John Knox. Above all, pray that God would raise up like-minded and like-hearted men in our own day, and once again give His Holy Spirit in great abundance to men who are deeply conscious of their own weakness."

—REV. IAN HAMILTON
Pastor, Cambridge Presbyterian Church
Cambridge, England

"Though I love John Knox, I rarely enjoy reading about John Knox. Most biographers leave me feeling like a pathetic worm beside this mighty lion of Scotland. But to my great surprise, this book lifted my spirits and even inspired me. Why? Because Douglas Bond has captured and communicated the secret of John Knox's power—a genuinely felt and openly confessed weakness that depended daily and completely on the grace and mercy of Jesus Christ. Mighty weakness—what an encouraging message for all worms who want to be lions."

—DR. DAVID P. MURRAY
Professor of Old Testament and practical theology
Puritan Reformed Theological Seminary, Grand Rapids, Michigan

"Another volume appears in the Long Line of Godly Men Profiles series, this time a profile of John Knox by Douglas Bond. To this very interesting book about a very interesting man, Bond brings his compelling narrative style, honed in his previously written novels. The preface ('John Knox: A Weak Man Made Mighty') sets the tone for the volume, as Bond demonstrates in a variety of ways how God took Knox's several weaknesses to make him one of the Reformation's strongest figures. Citing Knox's greatest strength in his submission to Christ, Bond then traces 'power' in Knox's life, whether it be power of prayer, pen, or predestination, or power in Knox's preaching. For those wondering whether the Pauline mystery of strength in weakness can become true for them, Bond's portrait of Knox will prove as edifying as it is instructive."

—DR. T. DAVID GORDON
Professor of religion and Greek
Grove City College, Grove City, Pennsylvania

The Long Line of Godly Men Profiles
Series editor, Steven J. Lawson

The Expository Genius of John Calvin
by Steven J. Lawson

The Unwavering Resolve of Jonathan Edwards
by Steven J. Lawson

The Mighty Weakness of John Knox
by Douglas Bond

The Mighty Weakness of

John Knox

A **Long Line of Godly Men** Profile

The Mighty Weakness of

John Knox

DOUGLAS BOND

℞

Reformation Trust

PUBLISHING

A DIVISION OF LIGONIER MINISTRIES · ORLANDO, FLORIDA

The Mighty Weakness of John Knox

© 2011 by Douglas Bond

Published by Reformation Trust Publishing
a division of Ligonier Ministries
421 Ligonier Court, Sanford, FL 32771

www.ligonier.org   www.reformationtrust.com

Printed in Crawfordsville, Indiana
RR Donnelley and Sons
June 2011
First edition

Cover design: Chris Larson
Cover illustration: Kent Barton
Interior design and typeset: Katherine Lloyd, The DESK

All Scripture quotations are from *The Holy Bible, English Standard Version*, copyright © 2001 by Crossway Bibles, a division of Good News Publishers. Used by permission. All rights reserved.

Library of Congress Cataloging-in-Publication Data

Bond, Douglas, 1958-
  The mighty weakness of John Knox / by Douglas Bond.
    p. cm. -- (The long line of godly men profiles)
  Includes bibliographical references (p.   ) and index.
  ISBN 978-1-56769-255-6
1. Knox, John, ca. 1514-1572. I. Title.
  BX9223.B55 2011
  285'.2092--dc22
  [B]

                          2011009264

To my wife

TABLE OF CONTENTS

Followers Worthy
to Be Followed

D own through the centuries, God has raised up a long
line of godly men whom He has mightily used at critical junctures of church history. These valiant individuals have
come from all walks of life—from the ivy-covered halls of elite
schools to the dusty back rooms of tradesmen's shops. They
have arisen from all points of this world—from highly visible venues in densely populated cities to obscure hamlets in
remote places. Yet despite these differences, these pivotal figures, trophies of God's grace, have had much in common.

Certainly each man possessed stalwart faith in God and
the Lord Jesus Christ, but more can be said. Each of them
held deep convictions as to the God-exalting truths known
as the doctrines of grace. Though they differed in second-
ary matters of theology, they stood shoulder to shoulder in
championing the doctrines that magnify the sovereign grace
of God in His saving purposes in the world. To a man, they

upheld the essential truth that "salvation is of the Lord" (Ps. 3:8; Jonah 2:9).

How did these truths affect their lives? Far from paralyzing them, the doctrines of grace inflamed their hearts with reverential awe for God and humbled their souls before His throne. Moreover, the truths of sovereign grace emboldened these men to further the cause of Christ on the earth. This fact should not surprise us, as history reveals that those who embrace these truths are granted extraordinary confidence in their God. With an enlarged vision of Him, they step forward and accomplish the work of many men, leaving a godly influence on generations to come. They arise with wings like eagles and soar over their times in history. Experientially, the doctrines of grace renew their spirits and empower them to serve God in their divinely appointed hours.

The Long Line of Godly Men Profiles aim to highlight key figures from this procession of sovereign-grace men. It is the purpose of this series to explore how these figures used their God-given gifts and abilities to further the kingdom of heaven. Because they were stalwart followers of Christ, their examples are worthy of emulation today.

In this volume, Douglas Bond introduces to us the Scottish Reformer John Knox. Knox's voice thundered throughout Scotland in a day when the church stood in great need of revival. Despite personal weakness and timidity, Knox was marked by stout faith in Christ. As the Lord empowered Knox's leadership, the Scottish "kirk" became one of the strongest expressions of the kingdom of God the world has ever witnessed. To this day, Knox remains the greatest of all Scots, eminently worthy to be profiled in this series.

As you read this book, may the Lord use it greatly to shape you like Knox, that you too might be one who leaves an indelible influence on this world. May you be strengthened to walk in a manner worthy of your calling.

Soli Deo gloria!

—*Steven J. Lawson*
Series editor

John Knox: A Weak Man Made Mighty

"John Knox felt toward [Scotland's] idolaters," wrote historian Roland Bainton, "as Elijah toward the priests of Baal."[1] Bainton's comparison of Knox and Elijah is an apt one. Elijah was called, by the express command of God, to draw his sword and cut down 450 deceitful priests of Baal (1 Kings 18:20–40). Men called to be prophets—to do feats such as Elijah was called to do—are not generally touchy-feely, kinder-and-gentler metro males. In redemptive history, the Elijahs have been tortured voices crying in the wilderness, lonely figures called to stand against teeth-gnashing critics, men charged with the profoundly unpopular task of declaring God's Word to people who have taken their stand with the enemies of that Word. Though he was not a biblical prophet, Knox was cast in this mold.

Is it mere hyperbole to say that "Knox was a Hebrew Jeremiah set down on Scottish soil"?[2] With the zeal of a Jeremiah, Knox thundered against the "motley crowd of superstitions" that infested religious life in sixteenth-century Scotland, for he considered his country's devotion to such errors to be far worse "than the idols over whose futility Hebrew prophets made merry."[3]

When God's messengers have mounted the rooftops to decry people's transgressions against Yahweh—Hebrew ones or Scottish ones—the multitudes have responded, not surprisingly, with rancor and violence. Elijah, for example, drew the wrath of Queen Jezebel. For his Elijah-like zeal, Knox is—like his spiritual, theological, and pastoral mentor, John Calvin— "as easy to slander as he is difficult to imitate."[4] As is the case for any mere man besieged by controversy in turbulent times and called to do significant things that affect the fortunes of many,[5] critics have found much in Knox to attack.

HOSTILITY AND NEGLECT

In his lifetime, Knox was denounced by regents, queens, and councils, and his effigy was hoisted high and burned at the Mercat Cross in Edinburgh.[6] Ridiculed as "Knox the knave" and "a runagate Scot," he was outlawed and forbidden to preach by the archbishop of St. Andrews, and orders were issued that he be shot on sight if he failed to comply.

Knox did not comply. Years later, a would-be assassin fired a shot through a window of Knox's house in Edinburgh, narrowly missing his mark.[7] Still Knox preached.

What of his legacy since his death in 1572? The English Parliament, 140 years after Knox's death, condemned his books to public burning. In 1739, George Whitefield was ridiculed for preaching "doctrine borrowed from the Kirk of Knox" (*kirk* being the Scottish equivalent of the English *church*). Perhaps more than any other, he has been portrayed as "the *enfant terrible* of Calvinism,"[8] and has been characterized in books and film, and at his own house, now a museum, as a "blustering fanatic."[9] Moderns dismiss him as a misogynist for his untimely treatise against female monarchs and for his unflinching stand before charming Mary, Queen of Scots, denouncing her sins and calling her to repent.

In 1972, the four hundredth anniversary of his death, it was decided that such a man as Knox was an inappropriate subject to commemorate on a Scottish postage stamp. As a crowning blow, the Edinburgh Town Council ordered the removal of the stone marking his grave, relegating his earthly resting place to obscurity under a variously numbered parking stall.[10] In my most recent visit to Edinburgh, the "JK" once legible on a small square marker was obliterated. As faithless Israel resented Jeremiah's prophecy of doom and destruction for her whoredom against the Lord, so, for the most part, Scotland has resented the life and ministry of Knox.

WHY JOHN KNOX?

However, Knox himself would have been little troubled by such neglect, even hostility. It seems to be an essential quality in truly great men of God that they care far more for the glory of Jesus Christ than for themselves, which is reason enough to examine closely the life of such a man as Knox.

Furthermore, when Knox is stripped of his God-given might and the thundering power of his calling, what remains is a mere mortal, a small man, "low in stature, and of a weakly constitution,"[11] one who, when first called to preach, declined, and when pressed, "burst forth in most abundant tears" and fled the room.[12] In this, too, he was like Elijah, who cowered in a hole, feeling sorry for himself and begging God to deliver him from his enemies—even *after* his judgment on the priests of Baal (1 Kings 19:1–8). Yet, by the grace of God, who alone makes weak men strong, Elijah and Knox lived lives that were characterized far more by power and influence than by weakness and obscurity.

The life of Knox, then, is not just for people who like shortbread and bagpipes, kilts and oatcakes. Neither is it just for Presbyterians or people whose names begin with Mac (or who wish they did). Knox is a model for the ordinary Christian, especially the one who feels his own weakness but who nevertheless wants to serve Christ in a troubled world. Knox is eminently relevant to all Christians who have ever been forced to come face to face with their own littleness.

Who has not felt deep within him that he was too simple a man with too little to contribute to so great a cause as that of Christ and His church? What young woman, wife, mother, grandmother, or aged spinster has not wrung her hands, fearful and weak against the enemies of her soul and the church? Who has not thought that his gifts were too modest, that others could serve far better, and that he was too frail and timid to help advance the gospel of our Lord Jesus? Or who has not felt that he was being unjustly maligned by critics, assaulted by the mighty, mocked and insulted by the influential? So it was for Knox, but as he wrote of the Reformation in Scotland, "God gave his Holy Spirit to simple men in great abundance."[13] His contemporary, Thomas Smeaton, said of Knox after his death, "I know not if God ever placed a more godly and great spirit in a body so little and frail."[14]

CONTENTMENT WITH WEAKNESS

The Mighty Weakness of John Knox is intended to be a practical biography. The first chapter is an overview of his life and legacy, while the following chapters investigate how he was transformed from weakness to strength in various dimensions of his character and ministry. These chapters examine Knox as a Christ-subdued man of prayer, as a preacher, as a writer, as a theologian, and as a shaper of worship, education, and public life in sixteenth-century Scotland and beyond.

So pull up your footstool—or wheelchair—and learn

from the mighty weakness of John Knox. Take heart, all who have cowered at the enemies of Christ and His gospel. Read Knox's life and resolve with the apostle Paul, "For the sake of Christ, then, I am content with weaknesses, insults, hardships, persecutions, and calamities. For when I am weak, then I am strong" (2 Cor. 12:10). Weakness, in Paul's theology of ministry, is an essential prerequisite to being used of Christ. The Almighty is in the business of raising up simple, frail, and little people, and empowering them to be strong in Christ. Though few will be called to champion the cause of reformation in an entire country, Knox's life teaches that the most timid saint becomes a formidable giant when strengthened by the almighty power of God in Christ alone.

I am grateful to Dr. R. C. Sproul, Ligonier Ministries, and Reformation Trust for their unrelenting commitment to getting the gospel right, and for their commitment to this profile series as a way of contributing to that high goal. Dr. Steven J. Lawson, series editor, has set the bar high with his volumes on John Calvin and Jonathan Edwards, and his work has been a source of inspiration and encouragement. I am grateful for his passion and leadership in the profile series.

I am equally grateful for the editorial skill and patience of Greg Bailey, director of publications for Reformation Trust. Greg consistently reflects the grace and beauty of the gospel as he generously misses nothing, and as he sends me back to check this source, recast that sentence, or consider slashing this or that entire paragraph. I have never been so warmly critiqued or so encouragingly scrutinized as when the e-mails started coming thick and fast from Greg. When he must uncoil his editorial whip, it never stings, but always feels as if it is wielded by a friend who never deviates from the ultimate goal of getting the gospel right, which for Greg includes getting every jot and tittle right. Partnering with him in this volume has been a delightful experience.

The brothers who make up Inkblots, our men's writing gathering, deserve my gratitude for their listening ears and critical comments, especially Doug McComas, the founder of the 'Blots. I am deeply indebted to my mother, Mary Jane Bond, who is the first to read almost everything I write, and who offers valuable proofreading and brings a lifetime of literary experience to her many comments and suggestions. I am also grateful to the Scots-loving Spear family, who read this volume and offered many helpful suggestions.

I am equally grateful to my colleagues at Covenant High School for their encouragement on this volume, and to Dick Hannula and the board for making church history central to our curriculum and for providing me with many opportunities for travel and research that have enriched my appreciation of John Knox.

Above all, I am deeply grateful for my wife, Cheryl, who supported me in writing this volume in many essential and loving ways.

CHAPTER ONE

Knox's Life and Legacy

O Lord Eternal, move and govern my tongue to speak the truth.[1]

—JOHN KNOX

Ironies began right away for John Knox. It has been said there was "no grander figure in the entire history of the Reformation in [Scotland], than that of Knox."[2] Yet he likely was born into a simple working-class family.

Almost nothing is known for certain of his early life, not even his birthday—or his birth year. The only thing historians agree about is that he was born sometime between 1505 and 1514 in Haddington, about seventeen miles east of Edinburgh. Knox wrote nothing about his early years, and the obscurity in which he was raised was such that no one else bothered to record much about it either.[3]

Neither do historians agree about where Knox was educated. Some insist that he studied under John Major at the University of Glasgow, while others maintain that he studied at the University of St. Andrews, it being in the ecclesiastic jurisdiction of his birthplace.[4] Either way, Knox likely was subjected to the popular educational sophistry of the time, which was preoccupied with speculative absurdity along these lines: Will all of a man's toenails clipped throughout his lifetime rejoin the man at the resurrection of his body?[5]

In all likelihood, Knox never completed his degree, perhaps because of such pedagogic nonsense; nevertheless, historical records indicate that he was ordained a priest in his twenty-fifth year. The next years are silent ones, from which he emerges bearing a two-fisted broadsword as a bodyguard for the intrepid preacher George Wishart.[6]

Of his conversion, we are left largely to speculation. Some argue that he was converted under the preaching of the friar Thomas Guilliame in 1543. Knox wrote little about it, though words he uttered on his deathbed hint that a certain biblical text may have been instrumental in his conversion. "Go, read where I cast my first anchor," he said to his attentive wife as he lay dying. She read from John 17:3: "And this is eternal life, that they know you the only true God, and Jesus Christ whom you have sent."[7]

Knox's world was a turbulent one. There was perhaps no place in sixteenth-century Europe more in need of reformation than Scotland. Iain Murray has described it as "a brutal, backwater kingdom, dominated by covetous, bloated clerics as well as by a corrupt civil power."[8] Yet God was providentially at work in this world. John Wycliffe's Lollards had proclaimed the gospel of Christ in Scotland since the late fourteenth century, and more recently, a zealous young nobleman's son, Patrick Hamilton, had preached Christ, for which he had been arrested, tried, and subjected to a gruesome six-hour burning before San Salvator's College in 1528. Martin Luther's teaching on justification by faith alone was making its way into Scotland by his books and pamphlets.[9] Devoted smugglers were spiriting English Bibles into Scotland by cartloads, and *sola Scriptura* and the Reformed gospel were penetrating the corrupt universities of the realm. Meanwhile, peasants were singing popular ballads exposing clerical abuses and celebrating gospel truth.[10]

PERSECUTION BEGINS

Medieval churchmen were not amused. There were few "bloated clerics" more corrupt than David Cardinal Beaton of St. Andrews. Beaton was a tyrant "and inquisitor, sumptuous and ruthless, with his guards and his ladies and his seven bastard children."[11] Determined to stamp out the rising tide of Reformation, Beaton influenced the passage of a savage parliamentary act against "damnable opinions contrary to faith and the laws of Holy Kirk."[12] To give the new policy teeth, on January 26, 1544, Beaton ordered four men hanged for breaking Lent and refusing to pray to saints. Not satisfied, he arrested one of the men's wives, a young mother, for the "crime" of praying in Christ's name instead of Mary's during her labor pains. Beaton's henchmen seized the woman's newborn infant and condemned the mother to public drowning.[13]

Meanwhile, Wishart ranged far and wide, preaching throughout the Lowlands of Scotland. Young men such as Knox began gathering around him, captivated by his gospel message. Nobles in Kyle, Cunningham, and Ayrshire welcomed the dauntless preacher; the Lockharts of Bar entertained Wishart and heard him preach in the barrel-vaulted hall of their ancestral keep.[14] In spite of Beaton's repressions, the Ayrshire neighborhood—from moorland farmers to the earl in his fortress—drank in the preacher's message of forgiveness and grace in Christ. Wishart gained a hearing as well from the Campbells in Loudoun Castle, just across the River Irvine, the earls of which had for several generations embraced Lollard Christianity and would later champion the Covenanting cause.

Enraged at the growing popularity of Wishart, Beaton sent out friar spies to infiltrate congregations thronging to hear the man preach. To give legitimacy to his schemes, Beaton spread rumors that Wishart was plotting an assassination attempt against the cardinal.[15]

As night fell on January 16, 1546, Wishart showed Knox, one of his zealous protectors, a letter he had received earlier in the day from some of the nobles of Ayrshire. The noose was tightening and, fearful of Beaton, they had decided not to risk another public gathering to hear Wishart preach. Bewildered, Knox observed the anguish of his mentor, recalling his frequent foretelling of "the shortness of the time he had to travail, and his death, the day whereof he said approached nearer than any would believe."[16]

Ordering Knox to hand over the broadsword he carried in the preacher's defense, Wishart "held comfortable conversation on the death of God's chosen children," led his followers in singing Psalm 51, expressed his desire that "God grant quiet rest," and then sent the young men away from him. When Knox protested, Wishart said: "Nay, return to your bairns, and God bless you. One is sufficient for a sacrifice."[17]

Near midnight, Wishart was arrested by Beaton's agent, the earl of Bothwell. He was thrown into the infamous Bottle Dungeon in St. Andrews Castle, then tried, convicted, and condemned to death by burning. Worried that supporters might attempt to rescue Wishart at the stake, Beaton ordered armed soldiers to surround the scene and, from the battlements of the castle, trained cannons on the crowd. Beaton then made himself comfortable, watching the spectacle from "the castle windows, hung with rich hangings and velvet cushions."[18]

"For this cause I was sent," Wishart said as the executioner chained him to the stake, "that I should suffer this fire for Christ's sake. I fear not this fire. And I pray that you may not fear them that slay the body, but have no power to slay the soul." Wishart then turned and kissed the executioner, saying: "Lo, here is a token that I forgive thee. Do thine office."[19] Wishart died prophesying the imminent downfall of the cardinal who gazed with satisfaction at the flames. It was March 1, 1546.

KNOX'S CALL TO PREACH

Knox had dutifully returned to his "bairns," the boys to whom he was a private tutor in the town of Longniddry. Hence, he was not in St. Andrews to witness Wishart's burning two and a half months after his arrest, but word of the tragic event traveled rapidly, stirring up many throughout Scotland "to damn and detest the cruelty that was used," as Knox records in his history.[20]

At this point, it was impossible for Knox to vacillate. It was known that he was a supporter of Wishart and that he had carried a broadsword in his defense. Unrelenting as Beaton was in his determination to stamp out reformation, there was great danger for any who had publicly supported it. Thus, Knox was a marked man.

For a time, he continued his teaching duties, instructing Francis and George, the sons of Hugh Douglas, and another young man, Alexander Cockburn. In the course of this teaching, Knox developed an informal catechism based on Scripture, and he began lecturing on the gospel of John. Others came to hear these lectures, and before long they developed into exhortations. One thing was certain to any who eavesdropped on those sermons: Knox was a preacher, one with particular gifts not unlike those of his late mentor. Soon men began to say, "Master George Wishart spake never so plainly, and yet he was burnt: even so will Knox be."[21]

Then word arrived that in the early hours of May 29, 1546, several noblemen's sons had finagled their way into St. Andrews Castle and had given the night porter a thump on the head and a dip in the moat in the process. One of Beaton's mistresses, Marion Ogilvy, had only just been let out the postern gate. The men burst into the bedchamber of the reclining Beaton. "I am a priest!" he cried. "You will not slay me!" In reply, James Melville called him to repent of the slaying of Wishart, "that notable instrument of God," and after calling him "an obstinate enemy against Jesus Christ," ran him through with his sword. Beaton's dying words were: "I am a priest. All is gone."[22]

The ill-prepared laird's sons attempted to secure the castle and negotiate with Mary Guise, the queen regent and mother of the young Mary, Queen of Scots. Meanwhile, the Castilians, as they were called, urged Knox to join them and be their chaplain. Though he had taken no part in the slaying of Beaton, Knox made no apology for rejoicing at "God's just judgments" on the fornicating tyrant.[23] He agreed to join the young men occupying the castle.

When he arrived, Knox began teaching his young charges in the castle chapel while the queen regent's army made ready to besiege the fortress. However, Beaton had left an unintentional boon to the young reformers now in control of his stronghold. Paranoid of vengeance from his many adversaries, Beaton had reinforced his palace into an impregnable castle and had sumptuously provisioned it to sustain all but the most prolonged siege.[24] Tensions mounted as Melville and his men wrote letters to Henry VIII begging for military support from the English crown, and Mary Guise petitioned the French court to send its fleet to support her army.

During this time, Knox was increasingly called to expand his private instruction of his students into public preaching to the entire castle garrison, which he declined out of hand, refusing "to run where God had not called him." However, determined to make Knox their preacher, one of the men at last spoke for them all:

In the name of God, and of his Son Jesus Christ, and in the name of these that presently call you by my mouth, I charge you that you refuse not this holy vocation, but that you have regard to the glory of God, the increase of Christ's kingdom, and the edification of your brethren . . . that you take upon you the public office and charge of preaching, even as you look to avoid God's heavy displeasure, and desire that he should multiply his graces with you.[25]

Hearing this exhortation, the man who one day would preach like a trumpet blast before monarchs, thundering without a tremor, broke into tears and hurried from the room. However, he finally accepted the call and delivered his first official sermon on Daniel 7:24–25, in which "he showed the great love of God for his Church," and how the true church hears "the voice of its own true pastor, Jesus Christ."[26] As he commenced the high calling that would so occupy the remainder of his life and ministry, Knox prayed, "O Lord Eternal, move and govern my tongue to speak the truth."[27]

DEFEAT AND ENSLAVEMENT

"England will rescue us."[28] So thought the zealous Castilians, but aging Henry VIII failed to come to the aid of Knox and the young reformers in the castle. Meanwhile, France sent a formidable armada, twenty-one heavily gunned galleys, and a vast army, and began bombarding the fortress from the sea.

Untrained though they were, the Castilians enjoyed a degree of initial success, nearly sinking a French ship with one of the castle's cannons. Gleeful, they boasted of their victory and of the thickness of the castle walls; Knox, however, predicted that the walls would crack like "eggshells" and that those who survived the siege would be carried off as prisoners.

Determined to crush her foes, the queen regent ordered "cannons royal," massive double-barreled pieces, to commence a ferocious barrage, which did, indeed, begin reducing the walls of the castle to rubble. Soon, Knox and the Castilians began to despair. Hemmed in by land and sea, outgunned by trained soldiers and seamen, the young men began desperate negotiations for their lives.

Finally, July 31, 1547, Knox and the Castilians surrendered to the French-backed forces of Mary Guise. Knox and the other survivors were transported in chains to the French fleet, then across the sea to Rouen at the mouth of the River Seine. There, the Scots prisoners were divided up; Knox and several others were sentenced to serve as galley slaves, each chained to an oar of a ship.[29]

Rowing in the sixteenth century was no Ivy League sport. Knox was "bound with chains, and treated with all the indignity usually offered to heretics, in addition to the ordinary rigors of captivity."[30] Nineteen cold, drenching months of bad food, putrid water, and backbreaking labor left their mark on his health for the remainder of his days. Like John Calvin, Knox would suffer throughout his life from kidney stones, insomnia, and other ailments.[31]

Through it all, he was tormented by French Catholics attempting to convert him. He recounts an episode that took place on the Loire River near Nantes, where French officers attempted to force him to venerate a painted wooden image of Mary. "Trouble me not," Knox said. "Such an idol is accursed, and, therefore, I will not touch it." At this, his persecutors "violently thrust it to his face, and put it betwixt his hands." Ever careless of temporal consequences, Knox took the idol and cast it into the river. "Let our Lady now save herself," he said. "She is light enough. Let her learn to swim."[32]

During his slavery, Knox made two voyages back to Scotland. On the second, as the ship lay at anchor between Dundee and St. Andrews, Knox was so weak with disease that others were certain he was about to die. Fearing that Knox had slipped into delirium, a fellow Scot slave, James Balfour, asked him whether he recognized where they were. "Yes, I know it well," Knox replied. "For I see the steeple of that place where God first opened my mouth in public to His glory, and I know, no matter how weak I now am, that I shall not die until I shall glorify His godly name in the same place."[33]

MINISTRY IN ENGLAND

In early 1547, Henry VIII died and his only son was crowned Edward VI, a boy king under the tutelage and influence of godly men such as Hugh Latimer. After more than a year and a half of negotiations, Protestant advisors in Edward's court managed to secure the release of Knox and the Scottish prisoners taken at St. Andrews. There was one exception: Melville, the first to strike Beaton with his sword, had died in a castle dungeon in Brest.[34]

In February 1549, Knox, free and back on English soil, was welcomed enthusiastically by leaders of reforming efforts under way in the Church of England. The Cambridge Reformation that had begun at the White Horse Inn was reaching its height with the preaching and writing of Latimer, Archbishop of Canterbury Thomas Cranmer, Nicholas Ridley, and others. They taught what Knox had been teaching: that redemption was perfectly accomplished by Christ, that while the Roman Catholic Church had "revived the kingdom of the law," nevertheless by the power of God, "the Reformation was now reviving the kingdom of grace."[35]

Paid a salary out of the royal coffers, Knox preached every weekday, and in 1551 he was invited to preach the gospel before Edward VI at St. George's Chapel, Windsor Castle. So warmly was his preaching received that the English offered Knox the pastorate of All Hallows, Bread Street, an influential pulpit in London, which he declined. Not to be put off, royal advisors presented Knox with the bishopric of Rochester, which he also declined. It was said of Knox, "No money could buy him."[36] Perhaps he agreed with Latimer that "the most diligent bishop in England is the devil."[37]

Knox was suspicious of bishops and of those who had power to install them, and he soon found himself in sharp disagreement with Cranmer. In the *Book of Common Prayer*, the archbishop had prescribed kneeling as a suitable posture for partaking of the Lord's Supper. For Knox, kneeling before the elements of the supper smacked of the medieval Mass, "a human invention."[38] He felt that kneeling too easily turned the elements into idols. "The moving of the body outward," as his mentor Wishart termed it, "without the inward moving of the heart is naught else but the playing of an ape and not the true serving of God."[39]

At last it was decided that Knox might be used best farther north, away from London and nearer Scotland. He was sent to Berwick-on-Tweed, a crossroads border city infamous for loose living and corruption. In accepting the post, Knox turned his back on an influential bishopric, on daily contact with men of rank and stature, and on the opportunity to preach before the king of England. Such a downward career move was roughly equivalent to moving from the position of chief executive officer of a bank to that of an entry-level bean counter. Many preachers today likely would see such a move as a great setback in their professional careers. But though Berwick-on-Tweed was on the wrong side of the tracks, the worldly folly of such a move eluded Knox.

He threw himself into his new duties with zeal, "publicly to preach the [gospel] of Jesus Christ, and to feed the flock, which He hath redeemed with His own blood, and has commended the same to the care of all true pastors."[40] The Spirit of God had prepared the way for Knox, and the firstfruits of his preaching was the conversion of Elizabeth and Marjory Bowes, the wife and daughter of the governor of Norham Castle, the latter of whom would become Knox's wife.[41]

Knox's preaching of the gospel of grace in Christ alone aroused the displeasure of the bishop of nearby Durham, Cuthbert Tunstall, the man who had snubbed William Tyndale more than thirty years before by refusing to help sanction an English Bible, even burning a pile of Tyndale's New

Testaments before St. Paul's Cathedral in London.[42] Such was the incompleteness of the English Reformation that a man of Tunstall's gospel hostility could retain his comfortable bishopric.

Knox was summoned to appear before Bishop Tunstall, where he gave a thundering Bible-alone defense, delivered fearlessly before ecclesiastics of every rank:

> O God Eternal! Hast thou laid none other burden upon our backs than Jesus Christ laid by His Word? Then who hath burdened us with all these ceremonies, prescribed fasting, compelled chastity, unlawful vows, invocations of saints, with the idolatry of the Mass? The Devil, the Devil, brethren, invented all these burdens to depress imprudent men to perdition.[43]

EXILE IN GENEVA

Precisely what would have happened to Knox at the hands of Tunstall was left to speculation by the untimely death of King Edward VI, "that most godly and virtuous king,"[44] as Knox termed him. Edward's death in 1553 was followed by the ascension of Edward's half-sister, Mary Tudor, who soon earned the title "Bloody Mary." An ardent Roman Catholic who may have never quite recovered from Henry VIII's divorce of her mother, Catherine of Aragon, Mary commenced the persecutions of Protestants for which she is infamous in history.

With characteristic directness, as if filling his lungs for a trumpet blast, Knox wrote of her rise to power:

After the death of this most virtuous Prince, of whom the godless people of England for the most part were not worthy, Satan intended nothing less than that the light of Jesus Christ utterly to have been extinguished within the whole Isle of Britain; for after him was raised up, in God's hot displeasure, that idolatress Jezebel, mischievous Mary, of the Spaniard's blood; cruel persecutrix of God's people.[45]

Knox fled for his life to continental Europe "with less than ten groats in his pocket,"[46] a near-penniless fugitive. His exile was made the more burdensome because it separated him from the woman he loved and to whom he was now betrothed, Marjory Bowes. During the dark years of Mary's reign (1553–58), when she burned 280 Christians, some of them Knox's close friends, he was at times near despair.

Calvin, the French Reformer, had heard of the refugee Scot preacher and warmly welcomed him to the work in Geneva, Switzerland. But his time there was not lengthy. On September 24, 1554, Knox received a call to become pastor of an English-speaking church in Frankfurt, and with Calvin's encouragement, he accepted. He soon discovered, however, that the Frankfurt congregation was dominated by those who insisted on an Anglican form of worship, and for Knox the central event of Anglican worship was little different from the idolatrous Mass of Roman Catholicism.[47] He had little patience for any liturgy, by whatever label, that did not place the preaching of the gospel of Jesus Christ at its center.

Some men create ripples. Knox created tsunamis. In the face of Knox's opposition to the Anglican liturgy, several leading English refugees in Frankfurt suddenly became loyal Englishmen, devoted to Mary's crown. Never one to mince words, Knox had referred to Mary as "Jezebel" and to her husband, Holy Roman Emperor Philip II of Spain, as "Nero." The English who were looking for a way to rid themselves of Knox plotted to betray him to one or both of these rulers. Fearing the fallout to their city of the tension, the magistrates of Frankfurt warned Knox of his danger and urged him to flee.[48]

In a letter to Knox, Calvin rejoiced that "in the management of the dispute [he had] been more courteous and tractable" than the English, but Calvin nevertheless exhorted him to appease those with "rankling feelings" or a "lurking grudge," and to "cultivate a holy friendship" with the English at Frankfurt.[49] Calvin then invited Knox to rejoin him and take up preaching and pastoral duties among the English-speaking refugees in Geneva. Ministering close by Calvin's side in Geneva, Knox learned more of *solus Christus*, the truth that salvation is by Christ alone, and how to pastor and preach in the humility of Christ. Along with his preaching duties, Knox in all likelihood contributed to the translation and study notes for the Geneva Bible.

Throughout his ministry, Knox considered Calvin his spiritual father, and he sought the counsel of the Genevan Reformer in correspondences. So influential was Calvin in Knox's life and faith that when he lay dying, he asked his wife to read Calvin's sermons on Ephesians to him.[50]

Knox's time in Geneva was life-shaping. He wrote, "It is the most perfect school of Christ on earth since the days of the apostles."[51] Still, Knox loved Scotland and ached to return: "I feel a sob and a groan, willing that Christ Jesus might openly be preached in my native country, although it should be with the loss of my wretched life."[52]

"Openly be preached" meant that, for Knox, a day of fierce conflict with the Scottish crown lay ahead. While in Geneva, he began forming his understanding of the roles of church and state, and he came to the conviction that a monarch was unfit to rule over civil matters if she openly condoned idolatry in the church. He consulted Calvin on whether the Scottish church might openly rebel against "a magistrate who enforces idolatry and condemns true religion." Calvin counseled restraint.[53] But in the cause of Christ and the gospel, "restraint" was not in Knox's vocabulary.

So not surprisingly, in 1555 (the same year that Bloody Mary burned his friends Latimer and Ridley in Oxford), when John Erskine of Dun, David Forrest, Elizabeth Adamson, and other Scots nobles pleaded with Knox to return to Scotland, dangerous though it was, he went home and began preaching openly.[54] It is difficult to imagine a more hazardous or fearless preaching crusade. Predictably, Mary Guise, the queen regent, saw Knox's open preaching as throwing down the gauntlet, but he stayed one step ahead of her henchmen. He wrote: "Our Captain, Christ Jesus, and Satan His adversary, are now at open defiance, their banners are displayed, and the trumpet is blown on both sides for assembling their armies."[55]

During this commando preaching crusade, Knox took the opportunity to marry his betrothed, Marjory Bowes. Meanwhile, the more the Roman Catholic clerics and the queen regent condemned his preaching, the more support he gained from Scotland—from men of rank such as the illegitimate brother of the queen, James Stewart, Earl of Moray, down to the lowliest crofters. When he was burned in effigy in Edinburgh, the marriage was complete: Scotland had found her earthly champion in Knox.[56]

Urged to return to Geneva, Knox continued his ministry alongside Calvin from 1556 to 1559, during which time he wrote his poorly timed *First Blast of the Trumpet Against the Monstrous Regiment of Women* (1558), a scathing denunciation of female tyrants. It was intended for Bloody Mary, but it was Mary's Protestant successor, Elizabeth I, who read it. To say that it did not ingratiate Knox to the new female monarch of England would be understatement.[57]

RETURN TO SCOTLAND

In 1559, Knox was summoned by the Lords of the Congregation, the Reformed-leaning nobility of Scotland. Taking leave of his friend and mentor, Calvin, Knox sallied forth once more to his homeland, where the queen regent readied her defenses for his return.

Knox burst on Scotland like a world-class sprinter when the gun sounds. Feeble in health though he was and surrounded by the French-supported army of the queen regent, Knox was nevertheless determined to preach Christ. "I cannot, in good conscience, delay preaching tomorrow, if I am not detained by violence," he wrote. "As for fear of danger to my person, . . . my life is in the hand of him whose glory I seek, and, therefore, I fear not their threats. I desire the hand and weapon of no man to defend me."[58] In the aftermath of Knox's sermons, men and women were converted to living faith in Christ by the power of the gospel, and statues of saints and of Mary were toppled.

Mary Guise, fatally ill, did her best to stop him, but the effect was like that of a hummingbird on a jumbo jet. Undaunted even by her efforts to halt him with military might, still Knox preached. The archbishop of St. Andrews threatened that if Knox preached, he would be shot on sight. Knox preached anyway, from Perth to Fife and beyond. As a result, the summer of 1559 saw an extraordinary revival spread throughout Scotland.[59]

In November 1559, the queen regent rallied her army and attacked Protestant forces and people at worship in Leith. Some were killed. Still Knox preached. Fourteen priests in St. Andrews renounced their popery, repented of their sins, and professed faith in Christ alone. Knox preached on, and thousands more were brought to a living faith in Jesus.[60]

In a world of hype, such as ours, church-growth experts wonder how Knox managed such success without high-tech glitz and PowerPoint. Knox himself provided the answer: "By God's grace, I declare Jesus Christ, the strength of His death, and the power of His resurrection."[61] Perhaps never before in one country were there so many converts to Christ in so short a time. Of the rapid spread of the gospel in Scotland under Knox's leadership, Calvin wrote: "As we are astonished at such incredible progress in so brief a space of time, so we likewise give thanks to God whose singular blessing is signally displayed herein."[62]

After Mary Guise breathed her last in July 1560, the Lords of the Congregation, nobles of the realm, and members of the Scottish Parliament rallied to Knox's banner and the Reformation gospel. They commissioned Knox to form a committee of theologians to craft a confession of faith, "the sum of that doctrine which they would maintain, and would desire that present Parliament to establish as wholesome, true, and only necessary to be believed and to be received within that realm."[63] In four days, Knox and his committee of five completed the Scots Confession, perhaps first heard echoing through the Great Hall of Edinburgh Castle before the assembled Parliament. It boldly declared, "Rebirth is wrought by the power of the Holy Spirit creating in the hearts of God's chosen ones an assured faith in the promise of God revealed to us in his word; by this faith we grasp Christ Jesus with the graces and blessings promised in him."[64] On August 17, 1560, an enthusiastic Parliament voted to approve the Protestant confession, thereby agreeing that Roman Catholicism, "the old system, was rotten to the core."[65]

Soon thereafter, eighteen-year-old Mary, Queen of Scots found herself a widow when her husband, Francis II, king of France, died suddenly.[66] Mary tearfully returned to Scotland to take up her royal duties and to restore her country to the pope—and to meet Knox for the first time. "Beautiful, self-willed, brilliant, with the hard brilliance of the diamond,"[67] she was counting on her feminine charm to pacify Knox, as it had other males, a monumental miscalculation that no doubt perplexed her in the struggles ahead.

There was yet another death in 1560 that had a profound effect on Knox. Marjory, his wife and the mother of his two sons, also died. Calvin wrote that "Knox's departed wife had no equal," and referenced her as his "most sweet wife."[68] Knox's grief, real as it no doubt was, remained private. He would remarry four years later.

Meanwhile, he pressed on, laying foundation stones for the Scottish church. "I will be of no other church except of that which hath Christ Jesus to be pastor, which hears his voice and will not hear a stranger."[69] In the Scots Confession and the two *Books of Discipline*, Knox laid a foundation for theology, worship, literacy, and preaching in Reformation Scotland. The next twelve years were ones of building and sometimes bitter fighting to bring the theory to fruition. Like the prophets of old, Knox was hated and feared by some, and honored and respected by others. But Knox was unmoved by either reaction.

BEFORE THE QUEEN

In his clashes with the queen, Knox never budged a whisker on the centrality of Christ and the gospel. When the spiraling folly of Mary's reign descended into love triangles, murderous plots, political schemes, and further defiance of Scotland's Parliament and the approved Reformed confession of faith, Knox never flinched. He said, "Madam, as right religion took neither original strength nor authority from worldly princes, but from the Eternal God alone, so are not subjects bound to frame their religion according to the appetites of their princes."[70]

Knox was a man of his age and could be vitriolic in denouncing those who opposed him, to which the queen reacted with dumbfounded silence or tears, depending on which best suited her objective at the moment. But one evenhanded Knox critic affirmed that, despite his thunderings, "on no one occasion do we find him influenced by selfish or venal motives. In this respect he stands alone, and pre-eminent over all men."[71]

Preaching Christ at St. Giles Edinburgh, contending with monarchs and weak-willed nobles, Knox tirelessly distributed "the bread of life as of Christ Jesus I had received it"[72] until his last sermon, preached November 9, 1572. Too weak to walk, he was carried to and from his pulpit at St. Giles. Pain was nothing new to Knox; he had lived most of his life with it. Nevertheless, he wrote: "The pain of my head and stomach troubles me greatly; daily I find my body decay. Unless my pain cease, I will become unprofitable."[73] In the excruciating days that followed, friends and supporters gathered at his bedside. "The time is approaching," he told them, "for which I have long thirsted, wherein I shall be relieved of all cares, and be with my Savior Christ forever."[74]

DYING IN THE LORD

He was correct. Monday, November 24, 1572, was a day of hearing his wife read John 17, "where [he] cast [his] first anchor," and 1 Corinthians 15 on the resurrection, to which he responded, "Is not that a comfortable chapter?" He also heard more read from Calvin's sermons on Ephesians. At last he sighed deeply and said: "Now it is come. Come, Lord Jesus, sweet Jesus; into thy hand I commend my spirit."[75] In the silence that followed, he was asked to give some sign that he was dying in the promises of the gospel. Knox lifted a hand heavenward, sighed again, and "without any struggle, as one falling asleep, departed this life."[76]

Two days later, Knox's body was laid to rest on the south side of St. Giles (at the time of this writing, under parking stall number twenty-three). From commoner to nobility, a vast crowd filled the streets of Edinburgh to pay their respects. The earl of Morton, the regent, is variously quoted as saying at his grave, "There lies one who in his life never feared the face of man."[77] As if to aid timorous Christians through the centuries, Knox's fellow minister, Thomas Smeaton, eulogized him by pointing to God's gracious activity on display: "I know not if God ever placed a more godly and great spirit in a body so little and frail."[78] Any Christian who has ever felt little and frail can take heart from God's gracious work in the life and ministry of Knox.

CHAPTER TWO

The Power of a Christ-Subdued Life

I sought neither preeminence, glory, nor riches; my honor was that Jesus Christ should reign.[1]

—JOHN KNOX

It is no coincidence that one hundred years after John Knox lived, Scottish Christians signed their names in blood in defiance of tyrannical usurpers of King Jesus' reign, covenanting to "uphold the crown rights of the Redeemer in His Kirk." In that act, and in the decades of brutal persecution that followed it, we see the legacy of Knox's uncompromising Christology imprinted on his countrymen. From the first page to the last of Knox's written works, the reader is brought relentlessly back to the source of Knox's greatness: Christ was at the center of every dimension of his life. It is this, and this alone, that made Knox mighty in his weakness.

Peel back the layers and read between the lines—there is never a hint of false modesty in the man; his statements about himself, good or bad, are corroborated by those closest to him. His was an age when one did not admit weakness; devouring lions crouched in wait to crush weak men. Yet Knox unabashedly admitted his fears: "I quake, I fear, and tremble." It was that honest admission of his frailty, and his corresponding reliance on Christ, that gave him such force against the enemies of the gospel. He was not posturing when he admitted his fears. Because he knew himself to be a man of inherent weakness, and because he was an honest, humble man, he could say without pretext, "I sought neither preeminence, glory, nor riches; my honor was that Christ Jesus should reign."[2]

When a man is so subdued by the grace of God in the gospel that such a self-assessment is, in fact, accurate, that man—love him or hate him—stands out in the crowd. Thus, Knox had preeminence in Scotland. Yet disproportionate to that preeminence, he had neither glory nor riches. He gained preeminence because, like so few, he did not seek it; he did not set out to rule his world for himself. There was no pretext when Knox wrote, "It has pleased His merciful providence, to make me, among others, a simple soldier, and witness-bearer, unto men."[3] As such, he bent every spiritual nerve of his existence "that Christ Jesus should reign."[4] Surrounded by men of higher birth and greater formal learning, Knox nevertheless emerged in 1559 as the undisputed leader of the Reformation in Scotland. He remarkably managed to do so without hipster apparel, video streaming, or social media. He was a mega-preacher in a world unencumbered by such a category. Yet he was a tender pastor, a simple shepherd guiding simple sheep to a profoundly great Savior. In all of this, despite his diminutive stature, about Knox there was an aura of grandeur and force that defies modern measure.

To assess him proportionately, we must turn our minds back again to the prophets of old—Elijah, Jeremiah, and the rest. For some, "His tacit assumption of the role of Old Testament prophet has made him appear as a mere fanatic."[5] The modern spin on ancient prophets is that they were raving monsters, tyrants wholly incompatible with the imagined enlightenment of our age. Therefore, many assume Knox was a religious tyrant, and, like all tyrants, a proud, ambitious monster, a steamroller forcing his will and way, whatever the price.

This unfair view of the prophets suggests inaccurate conclusions about Knox. The best historians, friends or foes, find Knox's character to be "without a trace of personal vanity, self-seeking, or self-exaltation."[6] And yet, he had contemporaries who called him the "trumpeter of rebellion,"[7] men who today would rank him among the most intolerant of men.

One need only turn to the words of Jesus to understand better how Knox gained such preeminence—but came to be so disliked by so many: "If you were of the world, the world would love you as its own; but because you are not of the world, but I chose you out of the world, therefore the world hates you" (John 15:19). The world hated Christ and so hates

His elect, His devoted followers—especially the ones God endows with a double portion of divine enabling. It is little wonder the world hated Knox.

LIFE AS A BATTLE

Where there is hatred, inevitably there is warfare. Knox's was a life of fighting and battle. As in mortal conflict, the stakes in this battle were high. He had seen many of his friends and mentors hunted, arrested, tried, and burned at the stake. Before his death, he would learn of the St. Bartholomew's Day Massacre, wherein, by royal decree, twenty thousand French Huguenots were slaughtered. Knox was called as a soldier "in the battle of the Lord,"[8] and he knew that the servant is not above his master and that soldiering in such a cause is costly.

In a sermon preached on Matthew's account of Jesus' temptation in the wilderness, Knox prepared his flock for mortal conflict with Satan, and still more for ultimate victory in Jesus Christ:

Methinks our Master Champion, Christ Jesus, provoked our enemy to battle: "Satan, thou gloriest of thy power and victories over mankind, that there is none able to withstand thy assaults, nor escape thy darts, but at one time or another givest him a wound: lo, I am a Man like to my brethren, having flesh and blood, and all properties of man's nature (sin excepted): tempt, try, and assault me. I offer you here a place most convenient—the wilderness."[9]

In the unfolding scenario with Satan, Knox proceeded with the imaginative skill of a master storyteller; he had Jesus lay out the rules of engagement and declare what the result would be when Satan would be "vanquished and confounded, and must be compelled to leave off from all accusation of the members of my body; for to them appertains the fruit of my battle. My victory is theirs, as I am appointed to take the punishment of their sins in my body."[10]

From this, Knox drew application for his flock and for himself: "What comfort ought the remembrance of these signs to be in our hearts! Christ Jesus hath fought our battle. He Himself hath taken us into His care and protection. However the devil may rage by temptations, be they spiritual or corporeal, he is not able to bereave us out of the hand of the Almighty Son of God."[11]

Knox considered it a "miraculous work" that God had chosen to "comfort the afflicted by an infirm vessel" and had raised him up to "suppress such as fight against His glory."[12] Weak and infirm though he knew himself to be—he referred to his decaying body as his "wicked carcass"[13]—he could engage in the battle because his life had been subdued by Christ and the gospel. His was no longer a life at war with God and His will and ways. He took his stand against rulers who, in defiance of the reign of God and of Christ, set about to subdue the world around them to their own will and way.

Hence, Knox's was a life of battle with nobles who cared more about gaining political power than advancing the gospel, and against the aspiring absolutism of queens and regents who cared more about their temporal pleasures than their eternal souls. Gazing at the political, spiritual, and cultural landscape, Knox said, "I see the battle shall be great, for Satan rages even to the uttermost." Well into the conflict, he later said, "I have been fighting against Satan, who is ever ready to assault."[14] Yet Knox was fearless and confident because, "although Satan appears to prevail against God's elect, yet he is ever frustrated of his final purpose."[15]

THE LAST BATTLE

We're tempted to detach from a man like Knox, to shuffle him off into irrelevant oblivion because his circumstances were so different from ours. Weren't his battles more manageable because his calling was so high and mighty, and because his life was so glamorous? After all, he wielded a real broadsword, endured a castle siege, and survived slavery in a French galley; he had audiences with a queen and preached before a king; he contended with the powerful and influential in the realm, dodged the bullets of assassins, and steered the ship of Reformation for an entire nation. Meanwhile, we're busy trying to balance our checkbooks and feed the kids.

Bear in mind that these glamorous adventures nearly killed Knox; they did ruin his health, and he was forced to endure life in almost constant physical pain. Such glamour may be overrated. Furthermore, unlike many of our conflicts and woes, Knox's battles had multiple fronts: queens, envious bishops, vacillating nobles, dubious allies, the cannons of the French, and lone assassins, all amid near-constant headaches, burning fever, and gut-wrenching illness. In a letter to John Calvin, Knox wrote, "I am prevented from writing to you more amply by a fever which afflicts me, by the weight of labors which oppress me, and the cannon of the French which they have now brought over to crush us." Nevertheless, Knox concluded his letter to Calvin with confidence in God: "He whose cause we defend will come to the aid of his own."[16]

Knox was mighty in spiritual warfare because his life was subdued by his Champion, King Jesus, who, true to His promises, subdues all His enemies. As Knox encouraged his flock at St. Giles Edinburgh hundreds of years ago, so he encourages you and me: "Christ's hand is so powerful, His mercy and goodwill so prompt, that He delivers His little ones from their cruel enemy."[17]

Full of compassion and fellow-feeling, Knox, the "simple soldier," wrote encouraging words to his English brethren suffering under the "Persecutrix," Bloody Mary. His words speak to Christians who suffer for Christ throughout time, in every circumstance, and in every place:

By the brightness of God's Scriptures we are brought to the feeling of God's wrath and anger, which by our manifold offences we have justly provoked against ourselves; which revelation and conviction God sends not of a purpose to confound us, but of very love, by which He had concluded our salvation to stand in Jesus Christ.[18]

Just as Knox's love and loyalty to "Christ, Redeemer, Keeper, and King, controlled and sustained him the whole of his 'long and painful battle,'"[19] so simple Christians, graciously subdued by their Redeemer, will never find Christ's sustaining might lacking. "I am weak, but Thou art mighty," wrote hymn writer William Williams.[20] Our mighty Lord Jesus comes in our defense, when the battle is most strong, and holds us with His powerful hand. Our King will gain everlasting victory—be certain of it—over His and our enemies. In the warfare of life, we must stand with Knox as he stood with Christ. Yet Knox shows us that there is no greater posture to prepare us for such standing than humble kneeling before God in prayer.

CHAPTER THREE

Power
of Prayer

When John Knox went upstairs to plead with God for
Scotland, it was the greatest event in Scottish history.[1]

—CHARLES H. SPURGEON

In 1909, on the four hundredth anniversary of the birth of John Calvin, civic and church leaders unveiled the Reformation Wall in Geneva, Switzerland. There stood Calvin and three other leading lights of the Reformation rising eighteen feet high along the ancient wall of the city. On Calvin's far left stood John Knox, and chiseled in the wall next to him were the words *Un homme avec Dieu est toujours dans la majorite*, or, "One man with God is always in the majority."

Many kings in the history of the world have insisted that they ruled by divine right, that their will was God's will, that they were corulers with the Almighty Himself. On a more mundane level, most of us have had the painful experience of knowing men who believed they were right and everyone else on the planet was wrong. (If we reflect soberly, we're forced to shudder; some of us have been those men.) Was Knox yet another swaggering example of this sort of arrogance? There is no middle ground in a statement such as "One man with God is always in the majority." When spoken about a man, it's true about him or it's false.

Strictly speaking, in the history of redemption there never has been just one man with God. Elijah thought he was alone, but God told him there were seven thousand who had not bowed the knee to Baal (1 Kings 19:18). Knox had a host of antagonists, but many supporters as well. Few would dispute, however, that Knox was the man on whom the slings and arrows descended in the battle for Reformation in Scotland.

What was it about Knox that made him so much the single man in a majority with God that four hundred years after his life it was carved in stone in Geneva? No doubt it was many things, but perhaps chief among Knox's God-given qualities was his sanctified understanding of his complete worthlessness unless he was on *God's* side, unless he was with God. Knox never saw himself as inducing God to be on *his* side. He knew he had to be brought to a posture of submission to the will of God in all things.

Furthermore, Knox knew there was only one conduit by which that could happen: "Your will be done, on earth as it is in heaven" (Matt. 6:10b). Put simply, Knox knew that without prayer he was "a dumb dog,"[2] a watchdog with neither bark nor bite, of no use to anyone. Knowing this about himself, he humbled himself and fell to his knees, submitting his will, mind, and tongue to God in prayer. But unlike most of us, he did not do this only when things became unbearable. This was the pattern of his life.

Those who knew him best called Knox "an eminent wrestler with God in prayer."[3] Most men are not. We think we can handle things; we believe we can do it on our own. Why do men drive around for hours rather than stop and ask directions? Asking directions forces us to admit that we don't know where we are. We must admit our weakness, humble ourselves, and request help. Men don't like doing this. Herein is the proof of Knox's humility. He knew his profound weakness. He knew how lost he was. So he asked God for directions, and, hence, became the quintessential man of prayer.

THE FOUNDATION OF KNOX'S PRAYER

In 1566, Knox prayed the following: "Thou has sealed into my heart remission of my sins, which I acknowledge and confess myself to have received by the precious blood of Jesus Christ once shed."[4] This, his confession of faith, was the foundation of his ministry and his confidence in his praying.

This did not come naturally to Knox. He was not great in the pulpit, the public arena, or the closet by natural giftedness and self-confidence. He was giving an honest self-assessment when he said, "I have rather need of all than that any hath need of me."[5] Unpretentious Knox did not fake words like these to feign humility and thereby ramp up his approval rating with his congregation. By the grace of God, Knox was beyond such self-aggrandizement. He had a real sense of his own powerlessness, so he prayed earnestly for God's power. As the apostle James wrote, "The prayer of a righteous person has great power" (5:16b). Humility showed Knox his great need of prayer, and his earnest praying brought down on him great power.

Words ascribed to Charles H. Spurgeon reveal the wide extent of that power: "When John Knox went upstairs to plead with God for Scotland, it was the greatest event in Scottish history."[6] Prayer was the engine that advanced Reformation in Scotland, and Knox was the foremost prayer warrior in the realm.

THE BEST SCHOOL OF PRAYER

Knox learned his theology of prayer in "the most perfect school of Christ," Calvin's Geneva. Calvin begins his grand exploration of prayer by pointing to the only Mediator between God and man:

> In Christ He offers all happiness in place of our misery, all wealth in place of our neediness; in Him He opens to us the heavenly treasures that our whole faith

may contemplate his beloved Son, our whole expectation depend upon Him, and our whole hope cleave to and rest in Him. . . . Whatever we need and whatever we lack is . . . in our Lord Jesus Christ . . . it remains for us to seek in Him, and in prayers to ask of Him, what we have learned to be in Him.[7]

Knox certainly heard Calvin preach and teach on prayer many times during his exile in Geneva, and he no doubt often heard Calvin praying. He probably heard Calvin declare that since men are "destitute and devoid of all good things"[8] in themselves, they should meditate on the providential kindness of God in answering prayer mediated through His beloved Son, and that the "measure of our feebleness"[9] is ample reason for us to put all our hope in His mighty arm to help us. Under Calvin's ministry, Knox learned that there is no "other way to petition God than through Christ who alone is the way," and that "Scripture recalls us from all to Christ alone, and our Heavenly Father wills that all things be gathered together in Him."[10] He saw how Calvin grounded the effectiveness of prayer on the mediation of the Son: "Therefore, Scripture offers [Christ] alone to us, sends us to Him, and establishes us in Him."[11]

Thus, when Knox felt overwhelmed by spiritual and political enemies, when all hope from earthly powers was exhausted, when all seemed lost for the gospel in Scotland, Knox prayed:

Seeing that we are now left as a flock without a pastor, in civil policy, and as a ship without a rudder in the midst of the storm, let Thy providence watch, Lord, and defend us in these dangerous days, that the wicked of the world may see that as well without the help of man, as with it, Thou art able to rule, maintain and defend the little flock that dependeth upon Thee.[12]

SURROUNDED BY PRAYING FRIENDS

Knox was also the product of praying friends, and he knew how much he needed their prayer support. In a letter to Calvin, August 27, 1559, Knox candidly admitted the physical afflictions that enfeebled him, the oppressive weight he felt from his ministerial duties to his flock, and the raw fear that gripped him because of the political upheavals that surrounded him. He concluded the letter by calling on Calvin to pray for him and for Scotland: "He whose cause we defend, will come to the aid of his own. Be mindful of us in your prayers."[13]

Another letter to Calvin, written by a Scots nobleman, reveals more of the central role Knox played in Reformation Scotland, and the important role played by others who prayed for him: "Our brother Knox has just been bereaved of his wife. He himself, feeble in body but robust in mind, never flinches from labors. His arrival in Scotland was very seasonable . . . I pray that the course of his life may be prolonged for years, that his service may profit his country and the church."[14] On April 23, 1561, Calvin wrote a warm, consoling letter to Knox, which concluded with a benedictory prayer: "May the Lord always stand by you, govern, protect, and sustain you by his power."[15]

Humble Christian that Knox was, he knew his great need of divine enabling, so he both prayed and sought the prayer support of others, something men in the flesh rarely do. Americans, schooled in Emersonian self-reliance, find asking for prayer an awkward, maybe even unnecessary, task. As noted above, seeking prayer is a tacit admission that we are not capable in ourselves, that we are desperately needy, that the arm of flesh is weak and ineffectual. Men don't like owning up to these realities, but prayer itself, and awareness of our need of it from others, requires an honest admission of the facts. Knox was one who owned up to the facts about himself. Because of his candid acknowledgment of his great need, he sought the aid of the God of the universe, and one way he sought it was through the prayers of fellow believers. Empowered by the Almighty, Knox became the single most significant force to be reckoned with in an entire country.

Yet it was not only Knox's friends and supporters who appreciated the wide-ranging effect of his ministry of prayer. According to historian John Howie, Knox's ardent enemy, the queen regent, Mary Guise, admitted that she was "more afraid of [Knox's] prayers than of an army of 10,000 men."[16] If every

Christian prayed like Knox, the Devil and his minions would melt like wax before the fire.

A GIFT FOR LOWLY SAINTS

In one of Knox's treatises on prayer, delivered to soldiers at the Berwick garrison,[17] he said, "Prayer is an earnest and familiar talking with God."[18] This is a succinct definition that makes prayer accessible to all. Knox saw that there is no place for elitism in praying. One needs no European PhD to be mighty in prayer. The lowliest saint may become unconquerable in prayer. Knox tenderly urged sinners to pray and to do so constantly with confident expectation of God's willingness and power to hear and to answer:

> Where constant prayer is, there the petition is granted. Let no man think himself unworthy to call and pray to God, because he has grievously offended his Majesty in times past; but let him bring to God a sorrowful and repenting heart, saying, with David, "Heal my soul, O Lord, for I have offended against thee. Before I was afflicted, I transgressed, but now let me observe thy commandments" (Ps. 41:4). To mitigate or ease the sorrows of our wounded conscience, our most prudent Physician has provided two plasters to give us encouragement to pray (notwithstanding

the knowledge of offences committed): that is, a precept and a promise. The precept or commandment to pray is universal, frequently inculcated and repeated in God's scriptures. "Ask, and it shall be given to you" (Matt. 7:7). "Call upon me in the day of trouble" (Ps. 50:15). "Watch and pray, that ye fall not into temptation" (Matt. 26:41). "I command that ye pray ever without ceasing" (1 Thess. 5:17). "Make deprecations incessantly, and give thanks in all things" (1 Tim. 2:1–2, 8). Which commandments, whoso condemns or despises does sin equally with him that does steal. For in this commandment, "Thou shalt not steal" (Ex. 20:15), is a precept *negative*; so, "Thou shalt pray," is a commandment *affirmative*. And God requires equal obedience of all and to all his commandments. Yet more boldly will I say: He who, when necessity constrains, desires not support and help of God, does provoke his wrath no less than such as make false gods or openly deny God.[19]

For Knox, prayer without ceasing was not an optional activity, reserved for power saints. Not everyone was called to preach and pastor, but every Christian was called to pray. It is the command of God, and it is the great engine of communion with God and the channel by which He pours out His blessings on men and nations.

Troubles as Goads to Prayer

So Knox prayed. Beset on every side by powerful enemies who wanted to silence him or, better still, take his life, Knox understood that great troubles often act as goads, causing us to despair in our power and to turn in faith to God's power:

> Trouble and fear are the very spurs to prayer; for when man, compassed about with vehement calamities, and vexed with continual solicitude (having, by help of man, no hope of deliverance, with sorely oppressed and punished heart, fearing also greater punishment to follow), does call to God for comfort and support from the deep pit of tribulation, such prayer ascends into God's presence, and returns not in vain.[20]

As we have seen, Knox was seldom short of troubles. When in the thick of battle, when driven from Scotland, when unable to preach the good news to his beloved countrymen, Knox pleaded with God to enable him once again to preach "heavenly religion" to the needy:

> Haste the time, Lord! At thy good pleasure, that once again my tongue may praise thy holy name before the congregation, if it were in the very hour of death. And albeit, that I have, in the beginning, appeared to play

the faint-hearted and feeble soldier; yet my prayer is, that I may be restored to the battle again. And blessed be God, the Father of our Lord Jesus Christ, I am not left so bare without comfort, but my hope is to attain such mercy, that if a short end be not made of all my miseries, by final death, which were to me no small advantage, that yet by him, who never despiseth the sobs of the sore afflicted, I shall be so encouraged to fight, that England and Scotland shall both know, that I am ready to suffer more than either poverty or exile, for the possession of that doctrine, and that heavenly religion, whereof it has pleased his merciful providence, to make me, among others, a simple soldier, and witness-bearer, unto men.[21]

Precisely because Knox saw himself as a "feeble soldier," he prayed, and because he had fallen to his knees "sore afflicted," and sobbed out his fears and petitions before the Almighty, he more effectively taught the feeble in his congregation to do the same.

PRAYING IMPRECATORY PRAYERS

Concerning the mighty in the realm who opposed the gospel and persecuted the church, Knox, the "simple soldier," could rise up like Elijah and pray in another tone:

Repress the pride of these bloodthirsty tyrants; consume them in Thine anger according to the reproach which they have laid against Thy holy name. Pour forth Thy vengeance upon them, and let our eyes behold the blood of Thy saints required of their hands. Delay not Thy vengeance, O Lord! But let death devour them in haste; let the earth swallow them up; and let them go down to the hells.[22]

For this kind of praying, Knox is often criticized as harsh and uncharitable. Yet when we open the book of Psalms we read, "Let death steal over them; let them go down to Sheol alive; for evil is in their dwelling place and in their heart" (55:15) and "Blessed shall he be who takes your little ones and dashes them against the rock!" (137:9). Such imprecatory prayers appear not infrequently as righteous men call on a just and holy God to vindicate His name and to pour out His wrath on His enemies.

These prayers do not appear only in the Psalms and prophetic books. Paul employs similar language in regard to those who distort the gospel by going back to the law: "But even if we or an angel from heaven should preach to you a gospel contrary to the one we preached to you, let him be accursed. As we have said before, so now I say again: If anyone is preaching to you a gospel contrary to the one you received, let him be accursed" (Gal. 1:8–9). Later, he employs imprecatory speech in a more graphic vein: "I wish those who unsettle you would emasculate themselves!" (5:12).

None of this bears any resemblance to professional wrestling pre-bout hate speech. The psalmists and Paul are speaking about the enemies of Christ, those who are settled in their defiance against God's person and His people. Theirs is a righteous indignation against those who are set on destroying God and His kingdom. Such imprecations, far from being calls for personal vengeance for personal wrongs, are accurate foreshadowings of what God the holy Judge will do to His enemies on judgment day.

Recall that Knox (like David and Paul) lived in a spiritual war zone, where the enemies of Christ and the gospel lurked on every side. Bear in mind the torture carried out by tyrants such as Cardinal Beaton and Bloody Mary. Recall the archbishop of St. Andrews' order that Knox be shot on sight if he preached Christ, and the assassination attempts made on his life. Remember Knox's friends burned alive in Oxford for their loyalty to King Jesus. The vindication of God's name and cause mattered more than anything to Knox, so he stood in defiance of those who flaunted their earthly powers and prerogatives against the Lord.

He was not unaware that even in his own day he was perceived as a thunderbolt, uncharitable and severe. He wrote: "I am not ignorant that many have blamed, and yet do blame, my too great rigor and severity; but God knows, that in my heart I never hated the persons of those against whom I thundered God's judgments. I did only hate their sins, and labored at all my power to gain them to Christ."[23]

We think our distaste for imprecatory prayers and statements in the Bible is an improvement in us, that it shows that we're more loving than men like Knox. I wonder. It may rather indicate how enervated we have become by capitulating to a tolerant age that no longer believes in the teeth-gnashing reality of the final judgment of God.

A LEGACY OF PRAYER

Knox's praying legacy extended for generations in Scotland. His youngest daughter, Elizabeth, married John Welch, a man, like his father-in-law, who became famous for his preaching and praying.[24] The Welch home was filled with "earnest and familiar talking with God," and it was always audible and often loud. Welch would rise in the middle of the night to pray, and Elizabeth, fearing he would catch cold, would rise and cover her kneeling husband with a plaid for warmth.[25]

Eventually, for declaring that Christ, not James I, was the head of His church, Welch was accused of high treason, arrested, and thrown into prison in London. The story is told of how Knox's daughter traveled from Scotland and somehow managed to gain an audience with the king on behalf of her husband. James I asked her who her father was. "Mr. Knox," she replied. "Knox and Welch!" he exclaimed. "The devil never made such a match as that." He asked how many children her mother and father had brought into the world and whether they were lads or lasses. "Three lasses," she answered (Knox had two sons by his first wife). "God be thanked," he cried, raising his hands for joy. "For had they been three lads, I would have had no peace in my three kingdoms." The king told her that if she would persuade her husband to submit to his authority over the church, he would let Welch go free. Elizabeth must have learned how to stand her ground from her father. She held her apron toward the king and said, "Please your Majesty, I'd rather have his head here."[26]

Her husband spent so much time kneeling in prayer on cold stone prison floors that in the last years of his life he lost all feeling in his knees. His praying grandson, the covenanter John Welch, great-grandson of Knox, was found after his death to have calluses on his knees as hard as ox horn.

ONE MAN WITH GOD

Fittingly, of such a praying man as Knox, it was carved in stone, "One man with God is always in the majority." But the grace of God in prayer is not a zero-sum game; it is never depleted through overuse; it is never over-harvested. Such are the glorious riches of the gospel that in prayer we may join men like Knox, and may all be that "one man with God." And, as with Knox, regardless of the measure of our feebleness, in prayer all God's children have the attentive ear of their heavenly Father and the unregulated might of His arm to deliver them in time of need. Our self-reliance, compared with this, looks puny indeed.

It is the singular man who has so communed with God in prayer, as Knox did, who is best prepared to step into the pulpit and preach to God's people with God's voice.

CHAPTER FOUR

Power
in the Pulpit

The person of the speaker is wretched, miserable, and
nothing to be regarded, but things that were spoken
are the infallible and eternal truth of God.[1]

—JOHN KNOX

"Preaching was almost unknown"[2] in the Scotland into which John Knox was born. One Roman Catholic critic of Knox and the "pestilent preachers" of the Reformation was forced to admit that most of Rome's clerics were "ignorant and useless men" who "devoured their revenues in luxury and neglected their duty." He concluded that Balaam's ass could have done a better job of preaching than these men.[3] One of the popular ballads sung by the peasants illuminates the problem: "The blind bishop he could not preach, for playing with the lassies."[4]

Knox had a high view of the office of preacher, but not of himself as a preacher.[5] He wrote, "The person of the speaker is wretched, miserable, and nothing to be regarded, but things that were spoken are the infallible and eternal truth of God."[6] In an age of professional scholars and celebrity preachers, these words sound odd, yet Knox does not seem to have been posturing. He had a genuinely low view of his preaching: "It hath pleased God, of his superabundant grace, to make me, most wretched of many thousands, a witness, minister, and preacher."[7] Analyzing Knox's style as a communicator, C. S. Lewis disagreed: "He thought himself a timid, temporizing, culpably gentle preacher. . . . One is tempted to say that no equal instance of self-ignorance is recorded until the moment at which [Samuel] Johnson pronounced himself 'a very polite man.'"[8]

Today we probably would try to boost Knox's self-esteem, and we'd counsel him to get in touch with the preacher within. But Knox was untroubled by his frank perception of himself as an unskilled preacher. He believed that the power of a preacher comes not from inherent gifting, studied eloquence, or academic learning (Knox never completed his university studies). It comes, he was convinced, from divine anointing. So Knox prayed that God would speak, not he. He wrote: "O Lord Eternal, move and govern my tongue to speak the truth."[9] Weak man that he understood himself to be, Knox knew that if God did not empower him and speak through him by the Spirit, he was a "vain shadow"[10] as a preacher.

Trusting the power of God, Knox laid out the goals of his preaching: "The end I proposed in all my preaching was to instruct the ignorant, to confirm the weak, to comfort the consciences of those who were humbled under the sense of their sins, and bear down, with the threatening of God's judgments, such as were proud and rebellious." He concluded that he "labored with all [his] power to gain them to Christ."[11]

KNOX'S PREACHING MINISTRY

Knox reluctantly began his preaching ministry when he was pressed into service as a chaplain during the siege of the Castle of St. Andrews. By popular demand, the private tutorials he prepared for his "bairns" developed into public exhortations from the Word of God. As we have seen, he was, in his flesh, a timid, fearing man; "I quake, I fear, I tremble,"[12] he said. But when he opened his mouth to preach, all timidity vanished. The year before Knox died, James Melville, a student at St. Andrews, described what happened when the feeble old man began to preach. Knox, he wrote, was "lifted up to the pulpit, where he behovit to lean at his first entry, but ere he had done with his sermon, he was so active and vigorous, that he was likely to ding the pulpit in pieces and fly out of it." Melville admitted that Knox's preaching made him "so to quake and tremble that I could not hold pen to write."[13]

Knox knew that many took offense at his preaching and that they attributed his vigor to hatred of his enemies instead of zeal for the gospel. In one of his sermons before Mary, Queen of Scots, he offered an explanation: "Without the preaching place, I think few would have occasion to be offended at me; and there I am not master of myself, but must obey him who commands me to speak plain and to flatter no flesh on the face of the earth."[14] Still, there is a sense in which Knox's preaching was motivated by hatred. As Iain Murray has it: "He passionately hated that which destroys souls. He hated the system which had blinded people to the necessity of faith and salvation by the blood of Jesus Christ."[15]

An ardent man, Knox was on fire when he preached, and it seemed never to occur to him to alter his message or tone when he stood before the rich and powerful in the realm:

> My words are sharp, but consider, my Lords, that they are not mine but they are the threatening of the Omnipotent. . . . The sword of God's wrath is already drawn, which of necessity must needs strike when grace offered is obstinately refused. You have been long in bondage to the Devil, blindness, error, and idolatry prevailing against the simple truth of God in your realm, in which God has made you princes and rulers. But now doth God, of His great mercy, call you to repentance before He pour forth the uttermost of His vengeance.[16]

As sheep heed the voice of their shepherd, people from all walks of life flocked to hear this message. After his release from the French galleys, Knox was called on to preach almost daily, "if the wicked carcass would permit."[17] This was no small feat for a man whose health was nearly destroyed. "The pain of my head and stomach troubles me greatly; daily I find my body decay," he wrote. "Unless my pain cease, I will become unprofitable. Your messenger found me in bed, after a sore trouble[d] and dolorous night."[18] In this condition, as minister of St. Giles Edinburgh, he preached sermons three or four times a week, each of which lasted up to three hours.[19]

There was nothing shallow or therapeutic in these sermons. There was nothing manipulative to evoke an emotional response. Knox understood the condition of his hearers because he understood the condition of his own heart: "For we are so dead, so blind, and so perverse, that neither can we feel when we are pricked, see the light when it shines, nor assent to the will of God when it is revealed."[20] Hence, for Knox, no gimmicks were needed. For his hearers to respond to the gospel in faith, they needed the transforming power of God's sovereign grace alone. And since the Spirit of God had chosen preaching as the means for the conversion of sinners, Knox preached.

CHRIST AT THE CENTER OF PREACHING

Knox's pulpit ministry is perhaps best summed up in his own words: "I did distribute the bread of life as of Christ Jesus I had received it."[21] Whether setting forth the gospel of Christ, encouraging the persecuted, or decrying idolatry, the goal of his exhortation was that Christ would have no rival in his hearers' hearts. One burning passion drove Knox: "I feel a sob and a groan, willing that Christ Jesus might openly be preached in my native country, although it should be with the loss of my wretched life."[22]

Christ, then, was the unrivaled center of Knox's message, and the Bible alone was his source for that message. He rejected the claimed authority of the pope over the canon and interpretation of Scripture, and argued that the inner testimony of the Spirit of God convinces believers that the Bible is the very Word of God. Hence, he employed the *lectio continua* method of expounding the biblical text phrase by phrase, finding clarity by "an appeal from a difficult passage to a plainer, clearer passage in Scripture itself."[23]

Knox did not merely go to the Bible to prepare his sermons; knowing his weakness without it, he daily fed himself the "strong meat which nurtured a strong man."[24] Using the Geneva Bible, the one he had helped translate and annotate, he read in the Old and New Testaments and the Psalms each day, reading through the entire book of Psalms every month. Moreover, knowing how important it was for him to be preaching to a flock that knew the Bible, he urged his hearers to be daily in the Word of God:

Dear Brethren, if that you look for the life to come, of necessity it is that you exercise yourselves in the book of the Lord your God. Let no day slip without receiving some comfort from His mouth. Open your ears, and He will speak even pleasant things to your heart. Let your young learn to praise the gracious goodness of Him, whose mercy has called you from darkness to light and from death to life.[25]

When Knox stepped into the pulpit to preach the Word of God, he opened with a half hour of calm exposition of the text before him. Thereafter, he became more vigorous. Though it is for preaching that he is known—especially thundering preaching—the texts of only two full sermons have survived the centuries. Scholars find bits and pieces in letters, notes, and Knox's summations in his historical account of the Reformation. Like John Calvin, Knox preached without notes or manuscript. His reason? "I did ever abstain to commit anything to writ, contented only to have obeyed the charge of Him who commanded me to cry."[26]

Although manuscripts of Knox's sermons are limited, the recurring theme of the final triumph of Christ Jesus and the gospel in Scotland is plainly evident. He knew that it would not happen by his might or by believers outnumbering the gospel's foes. "What was our force?" he wrote. "What was our number?"[27] Victory would come by the strength of Christ. He alone would at last prevail, and then the gospel of grace would reign in Scotland. This was not the wishful thinking of a social revolutionary. Knox knew that final victory over temptation and sin would come about through the transforming power of the gospel in the individual lives of God's children.

In one of his two surviving sermons, Knox preached on the text, "Then Jesus was led up by the Spirit into the wilderness to be tempted by the devil" (Matt. 4:1). He declared:

> [Those who are tempted should] judge not themselves by reason thereof to be less acceptable in God's presence. But, on the contrary, having the way prepared to victory by Christ Jesus, they shall not fear above measure the crafty assaults of the subtle serpent Satan. But with joy and bold courage, having such a guide as here is pointed forth, such a champion, and such weapons as here are to be found, we may assure ourselves of God's present favor, and of final victory, by the means of Him, Who, for our safeguard and deliverance, entered into the battle, and triumphed over His adversary.[28]

Here Knox labored to give confidence to his flock in their sanctification. There is no hint of sanctification being a condition of justification; he didn't point his flock to fear and obedience to the law. Rather, he showed them their champion Jesus Christ, and he called them to "joy and bold courage," because Christ their Victor had already triumphed over Satan, sin, and death. There are echoes of Calvin in

Knox's preaching: "Christ contains both [justification and sanctification] inseparably in himself. . . . He bestows both of them at the same time, the one never without the other. . . . In our sharing in Christ, which justifies us, sanctification is just as much included as righteousness."[29] As frequently as Knox preached the imperatives of the Bible, he faithfully taught that sanctification, the work of God's free grace, is as certain as justification because it flows from the finished work of Christ in the gospel.

Knox summed up his christological hermeneutic, the grand object of all his preaching, this way: "Always I praise God, that Christ Jesus is preached."[30] One hears echoes of Knox's Christology in some Scottish preachers today. While researching and writing this book, I had the privilege of hearing Scot-born pastor Ian Hamilton preach in Cambridge, England, on Psalm 88. Warming to his text, he made a statement that encapsulated Knox's view of Scripture and of preaching: "Christ is in every verb, in every noun, in every adverb, in every adjective, in every participle—Christ is in every syntactical device in all of Scripture."[31] Christ-centered preaching should not, however, be seen as a curious ethnic distinctive. Knox and Hamilton are in good company. Jewish Paul (who'd never heard of oatcakes or haggis) wrote that he went to pagan Greeks "in weakness and in fear and much trembling," resolving "to know nothing among [them] except Jesus Christ and him crucified" (1 Cor. 2:2–3).

CLARITY ON LAW AND GOSPEL

Christians bewildered by those who preach that we keep or forfeit justification by our obedience or disobedience to the law will find in Knox's teaching refreshing clarity on faith and good works, "on which men so readily and so fatally go astray."[32] Patrick Hamilton, the first martyr of the Scottish Reformation, laid a firm foundation for Knox here. From Martin Luther, Hamilton had made the greatest of all discoveries, that men and women do not earn or keep salvation by the works of the law. Hamilton imaginatively put the adversaries, law and gospel, in the ring to contend with each other:

> The law saith, "Where is thy righteousness, thy goodness, thy satisfaction?" The gospel saith, "Christ is thy righteousness, thy goodness, thy satisfaction." The law saith, "Thou art bound and obliged to me, to the devil, and to hell." The gospel saith, 'Christ hath delivered thee from them all."[33]

Knox clearly shared Hamilton's understanding of imputed righteousness and gospel freedom in Christ. In the following sermon excerpt, he lays out the role of the law as a schoolmaster that leads sinners to Christ:

> For by the law came the knowledge of sin . . . especially of idolatry. By the law came such a revelation of God's

will that no man could justly afterward excuse his sin by ignorance. So that the law, although it might not renew and purge the heart, for the Spirit of Christ Jesus worketh by faith only, was a schoolmaster that led unto Christ. For when man can find no power in himself to do that which is commanded, and perfectly understands, and when he believes that the curse of God is pronounced against all those that abide not in everything that is commanded in God's law to do them—the man, I say, that understands, and knows his own corrupt nature and God's severe judgment, most gladly will receive the free redemption offered by Christ Jesus, which is the only victory that overthrows Satan and his power.[34]

Making plain that good works are always the fruit and not the root of justification and of sanctification, Knox and his collaborators, in the Scots Confession, further defined the source and power of good works:

The cause of good works, we confess, is not our free will, but the Spirit of the Lord Jesus, who dwells in our hearts by true faith [and] brings forth such works as God has prepared for us to walk in. . . . For as soon as the Spirit of the Lord Jesus, whom God's elect children receive by true faith, takes possession of the heart of any man, so soon does he regenerate and renew him, so that he begins to hate what before he loved, and to love what he hated before.[35]

Acknowledging that, this side of heaven, there will be continual warfare between the flesh and the Spirit, Knox grounded sanctification not in the power of man but in the continual regenerating work of the Spirit of Christ in believers, preserving them through the power of Jesus Christ:

> But the Spirit of God, who bears witness to our spirit that we are the sons of God, makes us resist filthy pleasures and groan in God's presence for deliverance from this bondage of corruption, and finally to triumph over sin so that it does not reign in our mortal bodies. . . . But the sons of God fight against sin; sob and mourn when they find themselves tempted to do evil; and, if they fall, rise again with earnest and unfeigned repentance. They do these things, not by their own power, but by the power of the Lord Jesus, apart from whom they can do nothing.[36]

Knox readily affirmed that we owe absolute obedience to the law, but one can only imagine how liberating was his message of deliverance from sin and the curse of the law by the vicarious obedience of Christ, and how it must have thrilled Scotland, long held in bondage to law by a distorted gospel. Knox taught that the "Synagogue of Satan," as he termed the

Roman Catholic Church, had reconstructed a kingdom of law and that the Reformation was restoring the kingdom of grace. Sinners owe what they can never pay to the law, so Knox preached: "We are never able perfectly to fulfill the works of the law. . . . It is therefore essential for us to lay hold on Christ Jesus, in his righteousness and his atonement, since he is the end and consummation of the law and since it is by him that we are set at liberty."[37]

PREACHING AGAINST IDOLATRY

In his first public sermon, Knox preached from the book of Daniel: "And another [king] shall arise. . . . He shall speak words against the Most High, and shall wear out the saints of the Most High" (7:24b–25a). It was a sermon that introduced the twin objectives that would mark Knox's preaching for the rest of his life: He would rail against tyrants—political or ecclesiastical—who set themselves against the Most High, and he would tenderly call lost sinners to repentance and faith in Christ.

Knox commenced his exposition by showing "the great love of God for his church, whom it pleaseth to forewarn against dangers to come." He then proceeded to do what virtually all Reformers did—equate the Roman Catholic Church with the beast[38] and the pope with the Antichrist. Next, he set about to prove from Scripture the doctrine of justification, "that man is justified by faith only," and "that the blood of Jesus Christ purges us from all our sins." From this foundation he contrasted "the doctrine of the papists, which attributeth justification to the works of the law," and cited the apostle Paul, who called such teaching "the doctrine of devils."[39] From there he set out "to strike at the root, to destroy the whole," by exposing the idolatry of the central feature of medieval Christianity, the transubstantiation of the Mass.[40] For Knox, the Catholic Mass created an idol out of bread and wine, crucifying afresh the Son of God and setting up a rival god to Jesus. Knox firmly believed that idolatry of any kind was anathema.

It was for this reason that Knox locked horns with Thomas Cranmer over the English practice of kneeling to receive the bread and wine of the Lord's Supper. Knox was vehement that participants on their knees would inevitably venerate the elements, which, for Knox, led straight back to the idolatry of the Roman Mass. Hence, the inclusion of the "Black Rubric" in the *Book of Common Prayer*, warning congregants that kneeling to receive the supper should not make them think they were worshiping the elements. Like a prophet of old, Knox called his hearers to root out and destroy all such idolatrous practices, first in their own hearts, then in their streets.

Knox is often criticized for stirring up violence in his listeners because of a sermon he delivered "vehement against idolatry"[41] on May 11, 1559, in Perth. When he concluded his sermon, an exuberant listener hurled a stone at the image of a saint. The dam broke, and the "rascal multitude"[42] vented its outrage at their oppressors, the bloated clerics, and the false superstitions enshrined all about them. Iconoclasm had begun. Statues of Mary and the saints were toppled from their niches and crushed into rubble. For this, the queen regent declared Knox a traitor against her realm and prepared her army to retaliate.

Such a sermon, and such a reaction, offends modern sensibilities. But we must understand Knox within his historical context. Perth was the place where Cardinal Beaton had hanged four men for breaking Lent and had executed a young mother by drowning for praying in Jesus' name instead of Mary's. It is little wonder violence followed Knox's sermon decrying corrupt clerics and their idolatry.

One Scottish lord wrote of Knox's preaching in a letter: "I assure you the voice of one man is able in one hour to put more life in us than five hundred trumpets continually blustering in our ears."[43] Knox could rail with relentless power against "bastard bishops" with "idle bellies," and "bloody tyrants" who fed on the bodies and souls of the poor.[44] When taken out of context, Knox is dismissed as a fanatic and, as he himself acknowledged, "a great hater." He was, indeed, consumed with hatred at the outrageous corruptions of the false system of religion that held Scotland in servile bondage to superstition. He wrote, "I have learned plainly and boldly to call wickedness by its terms, a fig a fig, and a spade a spade."[45] But it was love and devotion to the truth of the gospel of grace alone through faith alone in Christ alone, and love for the poor, deluded lost of Scotland, that fueled Knox's thundering hatred against idolatry. Prior to June 29, 1559, the day Knox first stepped into the pulpit at St. Giles,[46] there were no fewer than forty shrines to the Virgin Mary and the saints crammed into the High Kirk in Edinburgh. Flanked on all sides by idolatry, Knox believed he had been given a divine commission to drive the idolmongers from his heavenly Father's house.[47] And so he did.

Knox also felt a commission from God to drive error and falsehood from the state—a state that coddled the false religion in the church. In vintage Knox lines preached before young Mary, Queen of Scots, he laid out a rationale for resisting civil authority, even by force of arms, should it come to that:

> If their princes exceed their bounds, Madam, no doubt they may be resisted, even by power. For there is neither greater honor, nor greater obedience, to be given to kings or princes, than God hath commanded. . . . So, Madam, with princes that would murder the children of God that are subjects unto them. Their blind zeal is nothing but a very mad frenzy, and therefore, to take the sword from them, to bind their hands, and to cast them into prison, till they be brought to a more sober mind, is no disobedience against princes, but just obedience, because it agreeth with the will of God.[48]

Knox never advocated political revolution as an end in itself, but he firmly believed that he had a divine calling to fulfill: "My travail is that both princes and subjects obey God,"[49] he said to the queen. Knox's zeal for the gospel convinced him that a single celebration of the Mass was worse for the deluded sheep in Scotland than giving them a cup of poison to drink.[50]

We smile and shake our heads; maybe Knox was a bit too fanatical. "Think how much more good he could have done if he had been more relational, if he had been more like us," we say. But meanwhile, what idols remain untoppled in our world today? Perhaps they remain comfortably on their pedestals because, unlike Knox, many ministers prefer delivering sophisticated and erudite lectures on the one hand and non-confrontative chats about community and culture on the other. Zealous to proclaim Christ alone, Knox called "a fig a fig, and a spade a spade" in his preaching. Inflamed with Knox's zeal, Scotland tore down her idols and smashed them.

The Power to Preach

Knox's preaching ministry was a microcosm of the mysteries of God's providence. God called a timid man who trembled in his boots at the thought of preaching and who ran from the room in tears when first called upon to do so. When a man feels in his own strength that he can do something, he tends not to cry out to God in prayer to enable him to do it. He believes he is already capable, so he sees no need to depend on God's strength. But this was not Knox the preacher. Knox, who never completed seminary, knew that if he was to fulfill his calling as a preacher, he desperately needed God's power. Weak in terms of physical strength, he turned from himself to find the vigor that comes only from God.

For Knox, preaching was all about proclaiming the evangel of Jesus Christ, giving good news to a world that for too long had heard only bad news. Yes, he thundered vehemently against idolatry in the pulpit, but he did so because he wanted his hearers to see Christ alone in all the Scriptures. He preached the free grace of the gospel because he wanted men not to depend in any degree upon the works of the law for their justification, an act of God's free grace, or for their sanctification, a work of God's free grace.

Knox the preacher, however, wrote none of his sermons down, and so, ironically, we have few examples of actual sermons he preached. But this is not to say that Knox wrote nothing. Just as he was mighty in the pulpit by the grace and power of Christ, so he was mighty with his pen.

CHAPTER FIVE

Power
of the Pen

*[Knox] had great powers of expression; he was not
only articulate, he was an artist.*[1]

—EUSTACE PERCY

"In twenty-four hours," wrote John Knox, "I have not four free for natural rest."[2] Not only was he almost constantly sick in body, he suffered sleep deprivation. Along with preaching three times as often as most pastors do today, Knox trained preachers, reformed worship and liturgy, petitioned monarchs, urged nobility, and guided public policy as it affected the church in Scotland. In addition to all that, Knox had to dodge bullets—literally—and was under constant threat from political forces fully capable of terminating his life at their royal whim.

With such a high-stress life, he was a man who desperately

needed a sabbatical, but he never got one. We read nowhere of Knox taking Marjory and the children to the beach. Hemmed in on every side, Knox pressed on in the power of God.

The apostle Paul faced much the same kind of bone-wearying ministry:

> But we have this treasure in jars of clay, to show that the surpassing power belongs to God and not to us. We are afflicted in every way, but not crushed; perplexed, but not driven to despair; persecuted, but not forsaken; struck down, but not destroyed; always carrying in the body the death of Jesus, so that the life of Jesus may also be manifested in our bodies. (2 Cor. 4:7–10)

Knox, too, was afflicted, perplexed, persecuted, and struck down. Yet, like Paul, he knew he was not forsaken. He understood that in the grand exchange, Jesus was forsaken by His Father so that he—like Paul and all weary and perplexed saints—never would be.

Somehow, amid his myriad tasks and multitudes of afflictions, Knox found time to write a great deal—everything from encouraging letters to theological treatises. As in his preaching, so in his writing, Knox wanted Jesus to be made manifest, and the Lord filled his writing with power in manifold ways.

History has painted Knox as a fire-breathing maniac, and maniacs are seldom regarded in a friendly light, let alone as gifted authors. Knox believed he had "a certain clumsiness in himself,"[3] but seems never to have taken time out of his busy schedule to worry about how he would be perceived in print. When a man's supreme concern is that the life of Jesus be manifested in his life, there's no time for navel-contemplative nonsense. But the best historians use superlative language to describe Knox as a writer and stylist. One has written: "[Knox] had a strong sense of the picturesque and an even stronger sense of the ludicrous. He had great powers of expression; he was not only articulate, he was an artist."[4]

It is universally accepted in the pedagogy of writing that the simple is preferred over the ornate, the authentic over the contrived. Long before the proliferations of books on writing and style, Knox had already mastered the art of simple written communication. In a letter to Sir William Cecil, a vacillating noble who had conformed to Bloody Mary's regime, Knox declared that "in the cause of Christ's Evangel you [should] be found simple, sincere, fervent, and unfeigned."[5] Knox practiced what he preached—his writings display passion, tenderness, and theological clarity.

PASSION: *FIRST BLAST* AND *FAITHFUL ADMONITION*

In Knox's most famous—or infamous—work, *The First Blast of the Trumpet Against the Monstrous Regiment of Women*, we find a sample of the persuasive force he achieved in his writing:

"For neither may the tyranny of princes, neither the foolishness of the people, neither wicked laws made against God, neither yet the felicity that in this earth may hereof ensue, make that thing lawful which He by His Word hath manifestly condemned."[6] Herein Knox establishes a cadence that gives irrevocable momentum, driving the reader to his point: God is sovereign over all authority.

Because of *The First Blast*, many historians dismiss Knox as a misogynist. Better historians, however, know that *The First Blast* was "not more violently phrased than was the fashion of the age," and Knox's argument that it was "monstrous" (meaning "unnatural") for women to rule men "was the universal commonplace of that age."[7] As John Calvin put it in a letter to Knox, government by women was "a deviation from the original and proper order of nature, to be ranked, no less than slavery, amongst the punishments consequent upon the fall of man."[8]

We can better understand *The First Blast* if we bear in mind that Knox lived in a historical moment when several notably violent women ruled in European realms: Mary Guise, the cannon-wielding queen regent of Scotland; Mary, Queen of Scots, a brutal assassin and husband murderer; Catherine de Medici, architect of the St. Bartholomew's Day Massacre that took the lives of twenty thousand Huguenots in France; and Bloody Mary herself. Hence, Knox wrote:

> Wonder it is that amongst so many pregnant wits,
> so many godly and zealous preachers as England did

sometime nourish, and amongst so many learned men of grave judgment, as this day by Jezebel are exiled, none is found so stout of courage, so faithful to God . . . that they dare admonish the inhabitants of that Isle, how abominable before God is the empire and rule of a wicked woman, yea, of a traitress and bastard. . . . We hear the blood of our brethren, the members of Christ Jesus, most cruelly to be shed, and the monstrous empire of a cruel woman . . . we know to be the only occasion of all those miseries.[9]

Knox always had to live with his *First Blast*. It was intended for Mary Tudor, the "cruel persecutrix"[10] of the church and ruthless executioner of many of Knox's friends and fellow Reformers. It arrived, however, in 1558, shortly after Bloody Mary's own death, when Elizabeth I was newly on the throne. However at odds with Mary's religion and politics, Elizabeth had one thing in common with her: she was a woman. Imagine the affront *The First Blast* gave her as queen of England. Knox became painfully aware of this. In a letter to Mrs. Anna Locke, on April 6, 1559, he wrote, "My *First Blast* hath blown from me all my friends in England."[11] The damage done was never fully repaired, though Elizabeth's political interests and Knox's ecclesiological ones oddly overlapped; Elizabeth had no interest in French Catholicism regaining a stronghold in the north of her empire. Shrewdly, Knox shifted his appeal to her political interests.

When Mary Tudor married Philip II, king of Spain, thereby forging an indissoluble bond with Catholic Spain, Knox penned *A Faithful Admonition to the Professors of God's Truth in England*. The evil Knox foresaw in this alliance inflamed him with zeal. As he saw things, everyone in the realm would suffer for Mary's folly. He wrote:

[By this marriage, has not Mary showed herself to be] an open traitress to the Imperial Crown of England . . . to bring in a stranger and make a proud Spaniard king, to the shame, dishonor, and destruction of the nobility; to spoil from them and theirs their honors, lands, possessions, chief offices, and promotions; to the decay of the treasures, commodities, navy, and fortifications of the realm; to the abasing of the yeomanry, to the slavery of the commonalty to the overthrow of Christianity and God's true religion; and finally to the utter subversion of the whole public estate and commonwealth of England? . . . God, for His great mercy's sake, stir up some Phinehas, Elijah, or Jehu, that the blood of abominable idolators may pacify God's wrath that it consume not the whole multitude.[12]

Elsewhere in the *Admonition*, Knox again referred to Mary as "Jezebel," for which he was accused of treason. There is no disputing that Knox's "dislikes are written large and legible on the pages of his book." But his careful critics seem to agree that his "quarrels were not personal ones, and they were never petty or unreasonable; they were with the men and women who were hinderers or enemies of the cause of God in the land."[13]

After reading and analyzing Knox's *Admonition*, C. S. Lewis wrote: "It might be supposed that to read a body of work so occasional, so little varied in subject-matter, and so fierce in temper, was a hard task. In reality, the surprising thing is that it is not harder. He has humor: in places he even has tenderness. . . . It is safe and dependable prose; a better prose than any (except Tyndale's) which we have met in this chapter." Lewis's literary stature and Anglican affiliation make his friendly conclusions about Knox all the more credible. He concludes, "It is not the style that keeps readers away from John Knox,"[14] leading us to conclude that it is the substance of what he wrote that readers cannot stomach.

TENDERNESS: *COMFORTABLE EPISTLES*

"[Knox's] writings were no literary exercises; they were political thunderclaps," wrote one historian. "[Yet] no man of that eloquent age was more eloquent." Knox, he added, even wrote passages of "tenderness and beauty worthy of St. Paul."[15] In his *Comfortable Epistles* to the persecuted Christians who were suffering under Bloody Mary in England, Knox displayed both of these modes.

First came the literary thunderclap:

A kingdom begun with tyranny and blood, can neither be stable nor permanent, but that the glory, the riches, and maintainers of the same shall be as straw in the flame of fire. Altogether with a blast they shall be consumed in such sort, that their palaces shall be a heap of stones (Isa. 22); their congregations shall be desolate; and such as do depend upon their help shall fall into destruction and ignominy with them.[16]

And yet, with his next stroke, he shifted to empathetic tenderness to comfort the afflicted:

And therefore, beloved brethren in our Savior Jesus Christ, seeing that neither our imperfections nor frail weakness can hinder Christ Jesus to return to us by the presence of His word; neither that the tyranny of these bloodthirsty wolves may so devour Christ's small flock, but that a great number shall be preserved to the praise of God's glory; neither that these most cruel tyrants can long escape God's vengeance; let us in comfort lift up our heads, and constantly look for the Lord's deliverance; with heart and voice saying to our God, "O Lord, albeit other lords than Thou have power over our bodies, yet let us only remember Thee and Thy holy name."[17]

He went on to use biblically informed reasoning with eloquence to encourage them in their suffering:

> O brethren, is not the Devil, the prince of this world, vanquished and cast out? Hath not Christ Jesus, for whom we suffer, made conquest of him? Hath He not, in despite of Satan's malice, carried our flesh up to glory? And shall not our Champion return? . . . Stand with Christ Jesus in this day of His battle, which shall be short and the victory everlasting! For the Lord Himself shall come in our defense with His mighty power; He shall give us the victory when the battle is most strong.[18]

THEOLOGICAL CLARITY: THE SCOTS CONFESSION

In 1560, Knox and his collaborators wrote the Scots Confession in a mere four days. Knox had already crafted a confession of faith during his earlier exile on the Continent, but while he drew from his previous work, the Scots Confession stands on its own. Though Knox referred to it in his preface as "brief and plain" because of the circumstances and the shortness of time under which the confession was written, it has remarkable clarity and scope, as seen here from Chapter 16, "The Kirk":

As we believe in one God, Father, Son, and Holy Ghost, so we firmly believe that from the beginning there has been, now is, and to the end of the world shall be, one Kirk, that is to say, one company and multitude of men chosen by God, who rightly worship and embrace him by true faith in Jesus Christ, who is the only Head of the Kirk, even as it is the body and spouse of Christ Jesus. This Kirk is catholic, that is, universal, because it contains the chosen of all ages, of all realms, nations, and tongues, be they of the Jews or be they of the Gentiles, who have communion and society with God the Father, and with his Son, Christ Jesus, through the sanctification of his Holy Spirit. It is therefore called the communion, not of profane persons, but of saints, who, as citizens of the heavenly Jerusalem, have the fruit of inestimable benefits, one God, one Lord Jesus, one faith, and one baptism. Out of this Kirk there is neither life nor eternal felicity. Therefore we utterly abhor the blasphemy of those who hold that men who live according to equity and justice shall be saved, no matter what religion they profess. For since there is neither life nor salvation without Christ Jesus; so shall none have part therein but those whom the Father has given unto his Son Christ Jesus, and those who in time come to him, avow his doctrine, and believe in him. (We include the children with the believing parents.) This Kirk is invisible, known only to God, who alone knows whom he has chosen, and includes both the chosen who are departed, the Kirk triumphant, those who yet live and fight against sin and Satan, and those who shall live hereafter.

In the first *Book of Discipline* that followed the confession, Knox laid out the three marks of the church: preaching of the Word, administration of the sacraments of baptism and the Lord's Supper, and church discipline.[19] In it, Knox further proposed that all land and property held by the Roman Catholic Church be forfeited to the Reformed church. This was too much for the aristocracy—nearly half of all land in Scotland was owned by the Roman Church. Finally, a compromise was reached. Two-thirds would go to the ejected Roman clerics and their patrons; the remaining third would be divided between Parliament and the Reformed church. Knox's reaction shows his wit: "I saw two parts freely given to the devil, and the third divided between God and the devil."[20]

Though the Treaty of Edinburgh, July 6, 1560, made clear that Parliament was to remain strictly out of the sphere of religion, Knox wanted a pure church protected by a pure government, wherein subjects as well as rulers submitted to the authority of the true church. Hence, from August 1 to 17, the Scottish Parliament deliberated, earls and barons, clerics and prelates, finally approving the Scots Confession and thereby abolishing Roman Catholic religion and making all its practices criminal offenses.[21]

RUGGED ELOQUENCE

One of the means by which God enabled a man like Knox to so radically alter the direction of an entire nation—its Parliament, its nobility, its monarchy, its church—was by his rugged eloquence. Perhaps he was so empowered because with his pen he followed his own advice to be "simple, sincere, fervent, and unfeigned."[22] As a result, Knox left behind a body of literature filled with an "abounding vitality that quickens it from the first page to the last."[23]

Hence, Thomas Carlyle, the Scottish historian, in a nineteenth-century lecture at the University of Edinburgh, urged students to read Knox. "If you look into Knox," he said, "you will find a beautiful Scotch humor in him, and a great deal of laughter. We find, really, some of the sunniest things come out of Knox that I have seen in any man." He called Knox's *History of the Reformation in Scotland* "a glorious old book, which I hope every one of you will read."[24]

In all of Knox's writings, there was no single subject on which he wrote more than the doctrine of predestination, on God the Father's electing love of unworthy sinners to salvation.

CHAPTER SIX

Power of Predestination

The doctrine of God's eternal predestination is so necessary to the church of God, that, without the same, can faith neither be truly taught, neither surely established.[1]

—JOHN KNOX

Critics of John Knox and his theology like to portray him as "the *enfant terrible* of Calvinism."[2] This is partly because he consistently taught that salvation is nothing less than God's electing grace pitched on unworthy sinners chosen from all eternity. Predestination was so much a part of Knox's message that more than 150 years after his death, Arminians criticized George Whitefield for preaching "doctrine borrowed from the Kirk of Knox."[3] It is fair to say that much of the enduring hostility toward Knox is rooted in his doctrine of predestination.

Knox's comprehensive treatment of predestination makes up fully one-fifth of his canon, with more space given to it than to any other doctrine. Recall that he wrote none of his sermons down, so scholars do not have a comprehensive collection of his messages from which to draw their conclusions. Nevertheless, throughout Knox's writings, predestination takes up proportionately as much space as, for example, the apostle Paul gave to the doctrine in his letter to the Ephesians. It seems Knox understood the centrality of predestination to the purity of the gospel, which is why the enemies of free grace in his day "most furiously raged against that doctrine, which attributeth all praise and glory of our redemption to the eternal love and undeserved grace of God alone."[4]

To be sure, in every age vainglorious people furiously rage against any doctrine that so strips them bare, exposing their wretchedness and their utter need for salvation from a God who alone can accomplish it for them. Theologians and preachers, without due vigilance, seem to revert to what Jonathan Edwards described as his immature perspective on predestination: "From my childhood up, my mind has been full of objections against the doctrine of God's sovereignty, in choosing whom he would to eternal life. It used to appear like a horrible doctrine to me."[5]

Yet, curiously, ours is not an age with very many vein-bulging public denouncers of predestination. On the contrary, today it is almost obligatory to affirm some measure of belief in the doctrine. It's almost as if everyone feels they ought to want to be a Calvinist.[6]

Since man's natural antipathy to the doctrine, his tendency to furiously rage at God's sovereignty, has not diminished, why the scramble to affirm a doctrine so detestable to fallen human nature? Perhaps it is because we have tweaked the definition and thereby fabricated a low-calorie Calvinism, a tofu version of predestination, a doctrine so bland that there's little left to rage about, a predestination we can all agree upon.

Knox, however, taught undiluted, high-protein predestination, having come to his understanding of the doctrine while in exile in John Calvin's Geneva. On his deathbed, Calvin declared that he would "live and die in this faith which [God] has bestowed on me, having no other hope nor refuge than in His predestination, upon which all my salvation is founded."[7] This was the conviction of the mature Edwards, who described how his mind was subdued to biblical teaching on the doctrine until it became a "delightful conviction. The doctrine has very often appeared exceedingly pleasant, bright, and sweet. Absolute sovereignty is what I love to ascribe to God."[8]

In an age that is increasingly focused on the here and now, when many look for ways to explain away or diminish predestination, a believer who loves all biblical truths, as Knox did, will delight in and adorn the doctrine.

PREDESTINATION
IN THE SCOTS CONFESSION

Knox never taught predestination as an end in itself and never used it as a club to beat up Semi-Pelagians. He was not smitten by doctrine, be it predestination or any other. He understood that predestination was not the *cor ecclesiae*, the heart of the church, the central dogma. For Knox, the *cor ecclesiae* was Jesus Christ alone. Yet he saw predestination as a doctrine on which many others found traction. It was important because it undergirded the entire soteriological structure; it was the theological rebar in the doctrinal foundation on which alone his flock could stand with unshakable confidence in the sole sufficiency of Christ.

We have already seen that in the Scots Confession, Knox defined the church as containing "the chosen of all ages, of all realms, nations, and tongues."[9] Elsewhere in the confession, writing about Christ being both God and man, Knox declared that the "wonderful union between the Godhead and the humanity in Christ Jesus" emanates from "the eternal and immutable decree of God, from which all our salvation springs and depends."[10] This idea of the decree of God to save sinners in Christ undergirds all of the confession, but it is defined specifically in Chapter 8, "Election":

> That same eternal God and Father, who by grace alone
> chose us in his Son Christ Jesus before the foundation

of the world was laid, appointed him to be our head, our brother, our pastor, and the great bishop of our souls. But since the opposition between the justice of God and our sins was such that no flesh by itself could or might have attained unto God, it behooved the Son of God to descend unto us and take himself a body of our body, flesh of our flesh, and bone of our bone, and so become the Mediator between God and man, giving power to as many as believe in him to be the sons of God; as he himself says, "I ascend to my Father and to your Father, to my God and to your God." By this most holy brotherhood whatever we have lost in Adam is restored to us again.

Notice how Knox's theology is never far from Christ: "[His] language rises into singular beauty and pathos when the work of the sacrifice of the Savior is the theme."[11] So christological is Knox that in this paragraph on the electing love of the Father, he immediately brings his flock to the Son.

Perhaps in Calvin's disciple, Knox, historical theology has a clearer connection between predestination and the glorious doctrine that has been manacled with an inglorious and misleading name—limited atonement. Knox lets us draw no other conclusion: election is particular, and the work of Christ, of rigorous necessity, is particular. He continues the above paragraph by adding, "He has given unto us his only Son to be our brother, and given us grace to acknowledge and embrace him as our only Mediator . . . because he was able to undergo the punishment of our transgressions and to present himself in the presence of his Father's judgment, as in our stead, to suffer for our transgression and disobedience." None of this would make sense if Christ died simply to make men savable and not to accomplish and apply the eternal, saving benefits of His atonement to God's elect.

Knox concludes in a finale of ecstasy, affirming that God's electing love in the redemption of Christ did "triumph, and purchase for us life, liberty, and perpetual victory."

A NECESSARY DOCTRINE

For many Reformed Christians, Knox sounds a bit too enthusiastic. They affirm predestination, of course, but it has become theological wallpaper. They seem to say, "Let's get on to more interesting matters." For them, the doctrine of election is a long way from the *cor ecclesiae*. To hear some, infant baptism, keeping the Mosaic law, weekly communion, or wearing a clerical robe is now the heart of the church. Many apologize for predestination as if they wish God had planned things without such an inconvenient doctrine. Some even look for clever ways to skirt it. One can hear a professing Calvinist preacher expound Ephesians and skip over 1:3–11 with the words, "Paul is merely introducing themes he will deal with later in the letter."

However, Knox biographer James McEwen makes no effort

to skirt Knox's doctrine: "It is unnecessary to apologize for the predestinarian strain in Knox's theology. It was his business to expound the Biblical faith, and the Biblical faith is predestinarian from end to end."[12] McEwen can hardly do less, for Knox himself argued that if we are to be truly humble, if we are to "be ravished in admiration of God's goodness, and so moved to praise," we must know and believe the doctrine of eternal predestination. For Knox, if one wants the gospel and true worship of God, eternal predestination is not an optional doctrine but a most necessary one:

> The doctrine of God's eternal predestination is so necessary to the church of God, that, without the same, can faith neither be truly taught, neither surely established; man can never be brought to true humility and knowledge of himself; neither yet can he be ravished in admiration of God's eternal goodness, and so moved to praise Him. And therefore we fear not to affirm, that so necessary as it is that true faith be established in our hearts, that we be brought to unfeigned humility, and that we be moved to praise Him for His free graces received; so necessary also is the doctrine of God's eternal predestination.[13]

Knox also believed predestination to be necessary for the building up of faith and the assurance of salvation:

There is no way more proper to build and establish faith, than when we hear and undoubtedly do believe that our election . . . consisteth not in ourselves, but in the eternal and immutable good pleasure of God. And that in such firmity that it can not be overthrown, neither by the raging storms of the world, nor by the assaults of Satan; neither yet by the wavering and weakness of our own flesh. Then only is our salvation in assurance, when we find the cause of the same in the bosom and counsel of God.[14]

Knox understood that faith is never established and unwavering assurance never comes from looking to ourselves. How different is this outlook from that of preachers who tell their flocks to look away from eternal election for their assurance, suggesting, "Look to your baptism," "Look to your good works," "Look to your feelings," or "Look to your membership in the visible church." Knox sent his flock to "the bosom and counsel of God," to "the eternal, immutable good pleasure of God," to a salvation that cannot be overthrown by "the raging storms of the world, nor by the assaults of Satan; neither yet by the wavering and weakness of our own flesh."

PREDESTINATION THAT WORKS

It is to be expected that Arminians will not appreciate Knox's predestination, but among those who insist they are Reformed there is a pseudo-sophisticated new Calvinism that has redefined and reduced predestination to "covenantal election," an election that can be forfeited by unfaithfulness. This doctrine of election comes disturbingly close to making sanctification a condition of final justification. Such an "election" is no ground of security in God's eternal decree and purpose; therefore, it can be no ground of Knox-like assurance or "firmity" of one's standing with God.

Knox knew nothing of this kind of double speaking about predestination. His was the sturdy Pauline election, the doctrine that launched the great apostle to the Gentiles into ecstasies of praise in his epistles: "Oh, the depth of the riches and wisdom and knowledge of God! How unsearchable are his judgments and how inscrutable his ways!" (Rom. 11:33). Election that is merely a covenant partnership, wherein God does His part but man determines his final destiny by his faithfulness and his obedience, is far from good news, and it evokes neither indignation, on the one hand, nor adoration on the other. Knox's predestination was good news because he pointed men to the gospel of free grace in Christ, the Redeemer who fully accomplished His Father's eternal purpose for dead, unworthy sinners.

Knox never wielded predestination as a club; he tenderly uncoiled it as a lifeline for the foundering lost. Perhaps the persistent human inclination to diminish election may be counteracted by more faithful preaching of "doctrine borrowed from the Kirk of Knox," who borrowed it from the apostle Paul, who borrowed it from the finger of God Himself. By it alone will we be "ravished in admiration of God's eternal goodness, and so moved to praise Him."[15]

The same tenderness that governed Knox's teaching and application of the doctrine of predestination can be seen in his ministry to a number of weak and needy groups within the Scottish kirk.

CHAPTER SEVEN

Empowering the Weak

Remember, mother, that Jesus the Son of God came not in the flesh to call the just, but to call sinners . . . with hope of mercy and forgiveness of God by the redemption that is in Christ's blood.[1]

—JOHN KNOX

John Knox had a vociferous tongue and, when provoked, as we have seen, he could lay on the invectives against wickedness and the enemies of Christ and His church. But it is important to observe that he reserved his thunder for the influential elite. For the commoner, however, Knox had nothing but compassion and patience.

Knox raged against murderous queens and immoral bishops because they used their power to oppress the poor and weak. He decried the Roman Catholic Church and the pope precisely because "the merchandise [traded by] that Babylo-nian harlot shall be the bodies and souls of men."[2] In other words, Knox berated Rome not only for its neglect of the eternal welfare of the people of Scotland but also for its disregard for their temporal lives.

By contrast, Knox deeply loved the needy, downcast souls in Scotland, and was prepared to risk his life to help deliver them from bondage to sin—and to sin's tyrants. Knox often expressed this compassion in epistles sent to encourage suffering Christians. In one, he rejoiced "that God's most merciful providence is no less careful this day over his weak and feeble servants" than He was over "His dispersed and sorely oppressed flock" in the days of the old covenant exile.[3]

Knox sought to encourage and help all who were needy, but he seems to have had a special compulsion to help women, pastors, and lay leaders in the church.

THE WEAKER VESSEL

Under tyrannical wickedness in any place and time, no one is more sorely oppressed than women. Knox is vilified as a man who hated women, but it was in his chaste love and care for women pining under fears and oppression that Knox was most pastoral and tender.

Nowhere is Knox's compassion seen more clearly than in his correspondence with humble women in his flock. For instance, Elizabeth Bowes, Knox's mother-in-law, was often afflicted with doubts and fears for her soul. His gospel consolations to her in letters are representative of his pastoral concern for all those under his care: "Remember, mother, that Jesus the Son of God came not in the flesh to call the just, but to call sinners, not to abide in their old iniquity, but to repentance . . . with hope of mercy and forgiveness of God by the redemption that is in Christ's blood." With these words, Knox breaks all the stereotypes about relations between men and their mothers-in-law. With love and compassion, he turns her from her frailty to Christ's perfection, helping her see that Jesus' imputed righteousness fully covered all her sins before the Father:

> Your imperfection shall have no power to damn you, for Christ's perfection is reputed to be yours by faith, which you have in his blood. God has received already at the hands of his only Son all that is due for our sins, and so cannot his justice require or crave any more of us, other satisfaction or recompense for our sins.[4]

In another letter, he comes alongside the weak and shows them by example how to find courage in the "sweet promises" of the Bible:

> The searching of the Scriptures for God's sweet promises, and for his mercies freely given unto miserable offenders (for his nature delighteth to show

mercy where most misery reigneth), the collection and applying of God's mercies, I say, were unto me as the breaking and handling with my own hands of the most sweet and delectable unguents, whereof I could not but receive comfort by their natural sweet odors.[5]

The first letter he wrote to his first wife, Marjory Bowes, was mostly a pastoral exhortation full of concern for the state of her soul. Like John Calvin, Knox recorded very little about his family life and relationships. In the few places where he does refer to his wife, it is as his "left hand" and as a helper in his writing. After she died in December 1560, he refers to his "heaviness by reason of the late death of his dear bed-fellow."[6] Her death left Knox to care for their two sons, a two-year-old and a three-and-a-half-year-old.

In one of his audiences with the queen, Knox's words reveal a tender father's heart, and an eloquent, though brief, snapshot into his family life: "I never delight in the weeping of any of God's creatures; yea, I can scarcely well abide the tears of my own boys whom my own hand corrects."[7]

On March 26, 1564, in one of the more controversial marriages of the Reformation, Knox, a widower in his fifties, married a distant relative of the queen, Margaret Stewart. She was seventeen. She bore him three daughters, Martha, Margaret, and Elizabeth; the latter would become the intrepid wife of John Welch.[8] Margaret Stewart cared for Knox in his final illness and was at his bedside when he lay dying, reading Scripture and sermons of Calvin at his request.

For the pompous who preyed on the feeble, Knox had nothing but thunder, yet it was thunder with a purpose.

Summoned to appear before Mary, Queen of Scots at her grand Holyrood Palace, Knox passed through the narrow streets of Edinburgh; on either side, the haggard poor were at their washing and meal preparation—women bearing loads, wearing rough clothing, caring for children. Ushered into the luxury of the palace, Knox was ordered to sit until the queen summoned him. While he waited, he observed the queen's four attendants, all named "Mary," "sitting in all their gorgeous apparel." Ever the preacher against vanity, Knox spoke:

> O fair ladies, how pleasing is this life of yours, if it should ever last, and then in the end you might pass to heaven with all this splendid gear. But fye upon that knave Death, that will come whether we will it or not! And when he has laid on his work, the foul worms will be busy with your flesh, be it never so fair and so tender; and the silly soul, I fear, shall be so feeble that it can neither carry with it gold, fine clothing, pearls, nor precious stones.[9]

Some might fault Knox for not appreciating the dressmaker's or jeweler's art. They might criticize his use of satire. But Knox, never the flatterer, simply went to the root of things.

He believed it was an act of compassion toward women to unmask the frivolity of the Renaissance court and point them to the realities of death and eternity.

EQUIPPING PASTORS

Repulsed by the vanity and ignorance of hireling clerics who had deceived and oppressed the ignorant poor of his homeland for centuries, Knox urged the Church of Scotland to appoint only "goodly and learned men" to her pulpits. He had no patience with a pastor who was a "vain shadow" of a servant of Christ. He believed a minister must be a pastor, a shepherd, who could "break the Bread of Life to fainting and hungry souls."[10]

Yet Knox was no elitist, setting about to create a sophisticated, intellectually respectable clergy, tempting though it may have been after the shameful abuses of the ministerial office throughout the Middle Ages. He knew this was not the way of Christ in His church, for He "came not to be served but to serve, and to give his life as a ransom for many" (Matt. 20:28). For Knox, no earthly minister-servant of Christ was above his Lord. Perhaps because Knox himself found such abundant strength in the midst of great personal weakness, he was used of God to raise up a comprehensive leadership of "simple soldiers," as he saw himself.

In a written prayer amended to the church order for the election and ordination of elders, Knox reveals the priorities and objectives of the office:

O Lord, Thou that art the Eternal Son of the Eternal Father, who has not only so loved Thy Kirk, that for the redemption and purgation of the same, Thou hast humbled Thyself to the death of the cross, and thereupon has shed Thy most innocent blood, to prepare to Thyself a spouse without spot, but also, to retain this Thy most excellent benefit in memory, has appointed in the Kirk, teachers, pastors, and apostles, to instruct, comfort, and admonish the same. Look upon us, O Lord, Thou that only art King, Teacher, and High Priest to Thy own flock.[11]

Perhaps Knox best revealed his view of the importance of the ministerial office as he handed off the two-fisted broadsword of his ministry, only days before he died, to his successor, James Lawson. He said: "And you, Mr. Lawson, fight a good fight. Do the work of the Lord with courage and with a willing mind; and God from above bless you and the church whereof you have the charge. Against it, so long as it continueth in the doctrine of the truth, the gates of hell shall not prevail."[12]

EQUIPPING THE LAITY

Stratified as society was in sixteenth-century Scotland, the common man, in matters either of state or religion, did not have a marginalized voice; he had no voice. The average person simply had no category for democratic ideas. Just as there were no ballots for political officers, so no church member in Scotland had ever nominated or cast a vote for an elder, deacon, or minister.

Under Knox's leadership, all that changed. The *Books of Discipline* declared that God showed no partiality toward people based on their birth or status, a biblical understanding that historian Kenneth Scott Latourette observed "furthered in the Scots a sturdy independence."[13]

Some persist in deconstructing Knox into a tyrannical steamroller, an ecclesiological Machiavelli. The best historians have concluded, however, that Knox's politics were, in fact, opposite to Machiavelli's pragmatism.[14] Knox didn't care about what some thought would work or not work in society. He cared supremely about the glory of God in Christ being worked into the very warp and woof of Scotland, which for Knox began in the heart of every man, woman, and child.

So, radically opposite to the Roman bishops, who scornfully predicted that every man "shall be a babbler on the Bible" and a "meddl[er] with the Scripture," Knox taught that "it is the duty of every Christian to seek the will of his God, and the assurance of his salvation, where it is to be found, and that is within his Old and New Testament."[15] But it was no small task to overturn centuries of determined effort to keep the common man cut off from the Bible.

One cultural theorist summed up the opposing paradigms this way: "To attract the poor to religion, one must either adorn the spectacle, as did the Catholics, or educate the people, as did the Protestants."[16] Medieval religion had worn itself out attempting to dazzle the masses with images and candles, vestments and ceremony, but Reformation Christianity was a religion of the Word, and Knox wanted that Word accessible to everyone. Rich or poor, male or female, he was determined that Christ's glory be known in all Scotland through literacy. Hence, he urged the nobility, "Of necessity it is that your Honors be most careful for the virtuous education and godly upbringing of the youth of the realm." He saw the grand objective of education as "the advancement of Christ's glory," and urged that Christ-centered education be established for the "continuing benefit of the generations following."[17]

To accomplish this, Knox, in the *Books of Discipline*, established the first national education system in the Western world. Hence, the prototype nation for universal literacy is Reformation Scotland, and every one of the "public" schools throughout the land—awkward though the fact may be to moderns—was distinctly Christian, with the Bible in English and "the catechism of Geneva"[18] as the curriculum.

Such a comprehensive invention of a literate society could not but have profound effects on Scotland. Whereas church members in the old system had been completely passive in worship—with the singing, the reading, the preaching, and the praying done for them, without their participation—Knox re-created worship along the lines of the days of the apostles.

In 1560, in *The Book of Common Order*, Knox described the order of worship: confession of sins, invocation of the Spirit of the Lord Jesus, singing of metrical psalms, and readings from the Old and New Testaments, followed by exposition, thanksgiving, and intercession—all in English, with the full participation of the people.[19]

Reformation historian Roland Bainton credits the wide-ranging "outreach of the church in the community" to Knox and his "unparalleled development of the lay leadership."[20]

Knox saw himself as a weak man made mighty by God's grace, a self-assessment that enabled him to see everyone else in Scotland in a hopeful light. One can only imagine the wide-ranging effects of this paradigm shift, both on those who had been in power and on the average layman, who was suddenly expected to take an active and meaningful part in worship and outreach. It was a change that would not have amused a bloated cleric or power-grubbing monarch: "The laity and the people were accorded a voice which monarchs were rightly to regard as a threat to their claims to absolute power." With the transformation, the common man in the church could hold office and exercise authority to a degree never before imagined. Latourette writes, "Provision was made on the parish level for the lay elder, and in the General Assembly which acted for the entire Church of Scotland." Under Knox's enabling and equipping of lay leadership, in the church "the rank and file had a much larger voice than in Parliament."[21]

AN UNSTOPPABLE SUPER-MAJORITY

For Knox, leadership in the church was not limited to "*One* man with God is always in the majority." Quite the contrary. His intention was to proclaim the good news and thereby bring along everyone in Scotland to be with God—members of His body, the church; partakers of the promises of the gospel in Christ; and part of His army, the church militant. With such a super-majority, the very gates of hell could not prevail against him.

Knox's insecurity in himself gave him the most profound confidence in the power of God to accomplish great things using ordinary men. Hence, small men throughout the realm were raised up by the grace of God and the power of the gospel to exercise their God-given gifts in the advancement of His kingdom. And what was true in the church became increasingly true in politics and culture, to the extent that it has been said, "Under God, John Knox was an architect of a Scotland enfranchised, intelligent, self-governing."[22]

CHAPTER EIGHT

A Legacy of Strength

[Knox's] works have not died. The letter of his work dies, as of all men's, but the spirit of it—never![1]

—THOMAS CARLYLE

What transformed John Knox from an obscure nobody, "low in stature, and of a weakly constitution,"[2] from a man "so little and frail,"[3] from a hand-wringing weakling who, when first called to preach, burst into tears and bolted from the room, into the indomitable thunderbolt, the theological earthmover of the Reformation, the "Hebrew Jeremiah set down on Scottish soil"?[4]

What was it about Knox that led English historian James Anthony Froude to conclude that there was "No grander figure in the entire history of the Reformation in this island, than that of Knox"?[5] What enabled such a constitutionally weak man to stand unflinching against political and ecclesio-logical tyranny? What enabled him to rally an entire nation, from peasant to parliamentarian, to stand unafraid before the enemies of the gospel? Why is it that historians say of such a man as Knox, "His was the voice which taught the peasant of the Lothians that he was a free man, the equal in the sight of God with the proudest peer or prelate that had trampled his forefathers"?[6]

There is but one answer. Knox was transformed from weakness to might by God's power. In this, Knox—and all who would be mightily used of God—was like Paul, who said, "When I am weak, then I am strong" (2 Cor. 12:10b). Because of this divine transformation, though Knox would roundly object, he is remembered by some in the superlative degree: "In purity, in uprightness, in courage, truth, and stainless honor . . . the spirit Knox created saved Scotland."[7]

"Now It Is Come"

I am writing these concluding thoughts on the second floor of Knox's house at Trunk Close on the Royal Mile in Edin-burgh. Surrounding me are audio reenactments of Scottish Psalter singing and of Knox preaching before Mary, Queen of Scots. His character in this reenactment is reminiscent of that of the mad scientist Dr. Emmett Brown (played by Christo-pher Lloyd) in the 1980s film *Back to the Future*. Meanwhile, the voice chosen for Mary, Queen of Scots is alluring and melodic—a soft, intelligent female voice. The verdict is in before the visitor has a chance to hear evidence and deliberate. Such a modern portrayal of the "altercation between the pretty girl and the trading reformer," observed Reformation scholar Roland Bainton, "evokes no sympathy for Knox in an age which has forgotten what it was all about."[8] Such a portrayal has much less to do with facts and far more to do with sentimental conclusions people persist in drawing about Knox and his female nemesis. But the romanticized picture is fatally misleading for any who care to know what, in fact, it was all about.

As I listen, my mind is carried back to November 24, 1572, when the man who often concluded his letters, "John Knox, with his one foot in the grave,"[9] lay dying. He asked his wife to read from John Calvin's sermons on the book of Ephesians. I can picture him in my mind's eye, lying on his bed in this room, his breath short, his face ashen, and his wife reading Calvin's sermon text: "Blessed be the God and Father of our Lord Jesus Christ, who has blessed us in Christ with every spiritual blessing in the heavenly places, even as he chose us in him before the foundation of the world, that we should be holy and blameless before him. In love he predestined us for adoption through Jesus Christ" (Eph. 1:3–5a).

I imagine Knox at 5 in the evening asking his wife, his voice barely audible, "Go, read where I cast my first anchor," and she reading from John 17: "This is eternal life, that they know you the only true God, and Jesus Christ whom you have sent. . . . I am not praying for the world but for those whom you have given me, for they are yours. . . . Holy Father, keep them in your name" (vv. 3, 9, 11b). Then I imagine Margaret turning to 1 Corinthians 15 and reading, perhaps with a tremor in her voice, "Christ has been raised from the dead. . . . In Christ shall all be made alive. . . . Christ the firstfruits, then at his coming those who belong to Christ" (vv. 20, 22–23). I hear the old man's whispered response: "Is not that a comfortable chapter?"[10]

John Knox—little and frail Knox—faced death the way he had faced the cannons of the French, the brutalities of the galleys, the hostilities of murderous queens, and the threats of proud prelates. "Now it is come," he said. Knox faced death with peace and resolution because he knew Christ Jesus had conquered death on his behalf. He died as he lived: trusting not in his frail and now rapidly fleeting strength, but in the perfection and righteousness of his Champion, King Jesus. Fittingly, his last words were, "Come, Lord Jesus, sweet Jesus; into thy hand I commend my spirit."[11]

"HONOR TO HIM!"

Scots historian Thomas Carlyle attempted to sum up Knox's life: "He had a sore fight of an existence wrestling with Popes and Principalities; in defeat, contention, life-long struggle; rowing as a galley slave, wandering as an exile. A sore fight: but he won it! 'Have you hope?' they asked him in his last moment, when he could no longer speak. He lifted his finger, pointed upward, and so died! Honor to him! His works have not died. The letter of his work dies, as of all men's, but the spirit of it—never!"[12]

Knox, no doubt, would thunder an objection: "Flesh of itself is too proud, and needs nothing to puff it up." His only claim, the sole thing in which Knox boasted, was "the free mercy of God in Christ."[13] Since he wanted all honor to be rendered to Christ alone, I suspect he would not think much of time spent writing or reading a biography given over to his life—unless it served as a means to point timorous souls to the greatness of Jesus Christ.

Knox's contemporary Thomas Smeaton understood the source of Knox's derived greatness: God by His grace and power made little and frail Knox into a great and godly man.[14] Hence, Knox serves as a model for all who know themselves to be little and frail, to be small and obscure, to be like Paul, who called himself "the very least of all the saints" (Eph. 3:8). From Knox's life, we can find encouragement to own up to our weaknesses and thereby find "strength to comprehend with all the saints what is the breadth and length and height and depth, and to know the love of Christ that surpasses knowledge, that [we] may be filled with all the fullness of God" (Eph. 3:18–19).

How can strength ever be wanting for the least saint who finds his might in the fullness of God's omnipotence? What might God do in our world if ordinary Christians acknowledged their frailty and found rest in God's grace and power?

Knox, the quintessential "simple, sincere, fervent, and unfeigned"[15] man, summed up what happened in his world: "God gave his Holy Spirit to simple men in great abundance."[16] May he do the same in our world. And may we be Christians, like John Knox, who know our mighty weakness, turn from ourselves, and find strength in the inexhaustible power of God alone.

* * *

For the sake of Christ, then,
I am content with weaknesses, insults, hardships,
persecutions, and calamities. For when
I am weak, then I am strong.
—2 Cor. 12:10

Time Line of John Knox and the Reformation

1512 First Reformation martyrdom in Paris

1514 (ca.) John Knox is born in Haddington

1516 Desiderius Erasmus publishes his Greek New Testament

1517 Martin Luther posts his Ninety-five Theses

1518 Ulrich Zwingli preaches in Zurich, sparks Swiss Reformation

1525 William Tyndale publishes English New Testament

1530 Lutheran Augsburg Confession is written

1534 Henry VIII decrees Act of Supremacy, break with Rome

1534 Ignatius Loyola founds Jesuit Order to renew Roman Catholic Church

1536 John Calvin publishes first edition of *Institutes of the Christian Religion;* Knox ends university studies, is ordained a priest

1540 Knox works as notary and private tutor

1543 Likely date of Knox's conversion to Christ

1545 Knox is supporter and bodyguard of George Wishart; Roman Catholic Council of Trent opens (concludes 1563)

1546 Wishart is martyred; David Cardinal Beaton is murdered in retaliation; Protestants storm St. Andrews Castle; queen regent puts castle under siege

1547 Knox joins Protestant Castilians and preaches first public sermon; castle falls to French; Knox begins nineteen months as French galley slave

PREACHING IN ENGLAND

1549 Knox is released and preaches before Edward VI; preaches in Berwick, England

1549 Thomas Cranmer's first *Book of Common Prayer* is published

1550 Mrs. Elizabeth Bowes and daughter Marjory are converted

1552 Knox disputes kneeling at Lord's Supper, declines bishopric of Rochester

1553 Edward VI dies; Catholic Mary Tudor ascends throne

REFUGEE IN EUROPE

1554 Knox flees to John Calvin's Geneva, pastors English congregation in Frankfurt

1555 Knox pastors English refugee congregation in Geneva, conducts commando preaching crusade in Scotland, marries Marjory Bowes

1556 Knox is condemned as a heretic in Scotland, returns to Geneva with wife and mother-in-law

1558 Knox writes *The First Blast of the Trumpet Against the Monstrous Regiment of Women*

1558 Mary Tudor dies; Elizabeth I becomes queen of England

REFORMATION YEARS IN SCOTLAND

1559 Knox returns to Scotland, preaches sermon condemning idolatry of Mass; revival and iconoclasm break out

1560 Reformation Parliament adopts Scots Confession; Knox's wife, Marjory, dies

1560 Knox helps write first *Book of Discipline*

1561 Mary, Queen of Scots returns to Scotland; Knox is minister at St. Giles Edinburgh, has first interview with Mary

1563 John Foxe's *Book of Martyrs* is published

1564 Knox marries Margaret Stewart

1566 Knox writes *History of the Reformation of Religion in Scotland*

1572 St. Bartholomew's Day Massacre in France

1572 Knox dies in Edinburgh, is buried near St. Giles High Kirk

The Scots Confession
of Faith

Author's note: Under the direction of the Scottish Parliament, John Knox and five colleagues (all named John) penned in four days the Scots Confession of Faith. On August 17, 1560, Knox and his fellow ministers presented the confession of faith to Parliament, then braced themselves for questions and debate. It consists of twenty-five brief chapters, each supported with biblical citations. The confession begins with the doctrine of God, and proceeds with affirmations about creation, original sin, the incarnation of Christ, election, the church, the Scriptures, the Holy Spirit, good works, the sacraments, the law, the life to come, and the relationship between the church and the state. As with other Reformed confessions, the person and saving work of Christ are the central themes of the whole confession. Though Roman Catholic clerics were present, there was little objection, and it was ratified by a significant majority of Parliament. Knox and his colleagues' work remained the confession of faith of the Scottish church until their rugged eloquence was superseded by the Westminster Confession of Faith in 1647.

Chapter 1—God

We confess and acknowledge one God alone, to whom alone we must cleave, whom alone we must serve, whom only we must worship, and in whom alone we put our trust. Who is eternal, infinite, immeasurable, incomprehensible, omnipotent, invisible; one in substance and yet distinct in three persons, the Father, the Son, and the Holy Ghost. By whom we confess and believe all things in heaven and earth, visible and invisible to have been created, to be retained in their being, and to be ruled and guided by his inscrutable providence for such end as his eternal wisdom, goodness, and justice have appointed, and to the manifestation of his own glory.

Chapter 2—The Creation of Man

We confess and acknowledge that our God has created man, i.e., our first father, Adam, after his own image and likeness, to whom he gave wisdom, lordship, justice, free will, and self-consciousness, so that in the whole nature of man no imperfection could be found. From this dignity and perfection man and woman both fell; the woman being deceived by the serpent and man obeying the voice of the woman, both conspiring against the sovereign majesty of God, who in clear words had previously threatened death if they presumed to eat of the forbidden tree.

Chapter 3—Original Sin

By this transgression, generally known as original sin, the image of God was utterly defaced in man, and he and his children became by nature hostile to God, slaves to Satan, and servants to sin. And thus everlasting death has had, and shall have, power and dominion over all who have not been, are not, or shall not be born from above. This rebirth is wrought by the power of the Holy Ghost creating in the hearts of God's chosen ones an assured faith in the promise of God revealed to us in his Word; by this faith we grasp Christ Jesus with the graces and blessings promised in him.

Chapter 4—The Revelation of the Promise

We constantly believe that God, after the fearful and horrible departure of man from his obedience, did seek Adam again, call upon him, rebuke and convict him of his sin, and in the end made unto him a most joyful promise, that "the seed of the woman should bruise the head of the serpent," that is, that he should destroy the works of the devil. This promise was repeated and made clearer from time to time; it was embraced with joy, and most constantly received by all the faithful from Adam to Noah, from Noah to Abraham, from Abraham to David, and so onwards to the incarnation of Christ Jesus; all (we mean the believing fathers under the law) did see the joyful day of Christ Jesus, and did rejoice.

Chapter 5—The Continuance, Increase, and Preservation of the Kirk

We most surely believe that God preserved, instructed, multiplied, honored, adorned, and called from death to life his Kirk in all ages since Adam until the coming of Christ Jesus in the flesh. For he called Abraham from his father's country, instructed him, and multiplied his seed, he marvelously preserved him, and more marvelously delivered his seed from the bondage and tyranny of Pharaoh; to them he gave his laws, constitutions, and ceremonies; to them he gave the land of Canaan; after he had given them judges, and afterwards Saul, he gave David to be king, to whom he gave promise that of the fruit of his loins should one sit forever upon his royal throne. To this same people from time to time he sent prophets, to recall them to the right way of their God, from which sometimes they strayed by idolatry. And although, because of their stubborn contempt for righteousness he was compelled to give them into the hands of their enemies, as had previously been threatened by the mouth of Moses, so that the holy city was destroyed, the temple burned with fire, and the whole land desolate for seventy years, yet in mercy he restored them again to Jerusalem, where the city and the temple were rebuilt, and they endured against all temptations and assaults of Satan till the Messiah came according to the promise.

Chapter 6—The Incarnation of Jesus Christ

When the fullness of time came God sent his Son, his eternal wisdom, the substance of his own glory, into this world, who took the nature of humanity from the substance of a woman, a virgin, by means of the Holy Ghost. And so was born the "just seed of David," the "Angel of the great counsel of God," the very Messiah promised, whom we confess and acknowledge to be Emmanuel, true God and true man, two perfect natures united and joined in one person. So by our Confession, we condemn the damnable and pestilent heresies of Arius, Marcion, Eutyches, Nestorius, and such others as did either deny the eternity of his Godhead, or the truth of his humanity, or confounded them, or else divided them.

Chapter 7—Why the Mediator Had to Be True God and True Man

We acknowledge and confess that this wonderful union between the Godhead and the humanity in Christ Jesus did arise from the eternal and immutable decree of God, from which all our salvation springs and depends.

Chapter 8—Election

That same eternal God and Father, who by grace alone chose us in his Son Christ Jesus before the foundation of the world was laid, appointed him to be our head, our brother, our pastor, and the great bishop of our souls. But since the opposition between the justice of God and our sins was such that no flesh by itself could or might have attained unto God, it behooved the Son of God to descend unto us and take himself a body of our body, flesh of our flesh, and bone of our bone, and so become the Mediator between God and man, giving power to as many as believe in him to be the sons of God; as he himself says, "I ascend to my Father and to your Father, to my God and to your God." By this most holy brotherhood whatever we have lost in Adam is restored to us again. Therefore we are not afraid to call God our Father, not so much because he has created us, which we have in common with the reprobate, as because he has given unto us his only Son to be our brother, and given us grace to acknowledge and embrace him as our only Mediator. Further, it behooved the Messiah and Redeemer to be true God and true man, because he was able to undergo the punishment of our transgressions and to present himself in the presence of his Father's judgment, as in our stead, to suffer for our transgression and disobedience, and by death to overcome him that was the author of death. But because the Godhead alone could not suffer death, and neither could manhood overcome death, he joined both together in one person, that the weakness of one should suffer and be subject to death—which we had deserved—and the infinite and invincible power of the other, that is, of the Godhead, should triumph, and purchase for us life, liberty, and perpetual victory. So we confess, and most undoubtedly believe.

Chapter 9—Christ's Death, Passion, and Burial

That our Lord Jesus offered himself a voluntary sacrifice unto his Father for us, that he suffered contradiction of sinners, that he was wounded and plagued for our transgressions, that he, the clean innocent Lamb of God, was condemned in the presence of an earthly judge, that we should be absolved before the judgment seat of our God; that he suffered not only the cruel death of the cross, which was accursed by the sentence of God; but also that he suffered for a season the wrath of his Father which sinners had deserved. But yet we avow that he remained the only, well beloved, and blessed Son of his Father even in the midst of his anguish and torment which he suffered in body and soul to make full atonement for the sins of his people. From this we confess and avow that there remains no other sacrifice for sin; if any affirm so, we do not hesitate to say that they are blasphemers against Christ's death and the everlasting atonement thereby purchased for us.

Chapter 10—The Resurrection

We undoubtedly believe, since it was impossible that the sorrows of death should retain in bondage the Author of life, that our Lord Jesus crucified, dead, and buried, who descended into hell, did rise again for our justification, and the destruction of him who was the author of death and its bondage. We know that his resurrection was confirmed by the testimony of his enemies, and by the resurrection of the dead, whose sepulchers did open, and they did rise and appear to many within the city of Jerusalem. It was also confirmed by the testimony of his angels, and by the senses and judgment of his apostles and of others, who had conversation, and did eat and drink with him after his resurrection.

Chapter 11—The Ascension

We do not doubt but that the selfsame body which was born of the virgin, was crucified, dead, and buried, and which did rise again, did ascend into the heavens, for the accomplishment of all things, where in our name and for our comfort he has received all power in heaven and earth, where he sits at the right hand of the Father, having received his kingdom, the only advocate and mediator for us. Which glory, honor, and prerogative, he alone amongst the brethren shall possess till all his enemies are made his footstool, as we undoubtedly believe they shall be in the Last Judgment. We believe that the same Lord Jesus shall visibly return for this Last Judgment as he was seen to ascend. And then, we firmly believe, the time of refreshing and restitution of all things shall come, so that those who from the beginning have suffered violence, injury, and wrong, for righteousness' sake, shall inherit that blessed immortality promised them from the beginning.

But, on the other hand, the stubborn, disobedient, cruel persecutors, filthy persons, idolaters, and all sorts of the unbelieving, shall be cast into the dungeon of utter darkness, where their worm shall not die, nor their fire be quenched. The remembrance of that day, and of the Judgment to be executed in it, is not only a bridle by which our carnal lusts are restrained but also such inestimable comfort that neither the threatening of worldly princes, nor the fear of present danger or of temporal death, may move us to renounce and forsake that blessed society which we, the members, have with our Head and only Mediator, Christ Jesus: whom we confess and avow to be the promised Messiah, the only Head of his Kirk, our just Lawgiver, our only High Priest, Advocate, and Mediator. To which honors and offices, if man or angel presume to intrude themselves, we utterly detest and abhor them, as blasphemous to our sovereign and supreme Governor, Christ Jesus.

Chapter 12—Faith in the Holy Ghost

Our faith and its assurance do not proceed from flesh and blood, that is to say, from natural powers within us, but are the inspiration of the Holy Ghost; whom we confess to be God, equal with the Father and with his Son, who sanctifies us, and brings us into all truth by his own working, without whom we should remain forever enemies to God and ignorant of his Son, Christ Jesus. For by nature we are so dead, blind, and perverse, that neither can we feel when we are pricked, see the light when it shines, nor assent to the will of God when it is revealed, unless the Spirit of the Lord Jesus quicken that which is dead, remove the darkness from our minds, and bow our stubborn hearts to the obedience of his blessed will. And so, as we confess that God the Father created us when we were not, as his Son our Lord Jesus redeemed us when we were enemies to him, so also do we confess that the Holy Ghost does sanctify and regenerate us, without respect to any merit proceeding from us, be it before or after our regeneration. To put this even more plainly; as we willingly disclaim any honor and glory from our own creation and redemption, so do we willingly also for our regeneration and sanctification; for by ourselves we are not capable of thinking one good thought, but he who has begun the work in us alone continues us in it, to the praise and glory of his undeserved grace.

Chapter 13—The Cause of Good Works

The cause of good works, we confess, is not our free will, but the Spirit of the Lord Jesus, who dwells in our hearts by true faith, brings forth such works as God has prepared for us to walk in. For we most boldly affirm that it is blasphemy to say that Christ abides in the hearts of those in whom is no spirit of sanctification. Therefore we do not hesitate to affirm that murderers, oppressors, cruel persecutors, adulterers, filthy persons, idolaters, drunkards, thieves, and all workers of iniquity, have neither true faith nor anything of the Spirit of the Lord Jesus, so long as they obstinately continue in wickedness. For as soon as the Spirit of the Lord Jesus, whom God's chosen children receive by true faith, takes possession of the heart of any man, so soon does he regenerate and renew him, so that he begins to hate what before he loved, and to love what he hated before. Thence comes that continual battle which is between the flesh and Spirit in God's children, while the flesh and the natural man, being corrupt, lust for things pleasant and delightful to themselves, are envious in adversity and proud in prosperity, and every moment prone and ready to offend the majesty of God. But the Spirit of God, who bears witness to our spirit that we are the sons of God, makes us resist filthy pleasures and groan in God's presence for deliverance from this bondage of corruption, and finally to triumph over sin so that it does not reign in our mortal bodies. Other men do not share this conflict since they do not have God's Spirit, but they readily follow and obey sin and feel no regrets, since they act as the devil and their corrupt nature urge. But the sons of God fight against sin; sob and mourn when they find themselves tempted to do evil; and, if they fall, rise again with earnest and unfeigned repentance. They do these things, not by their own power, but by the power of the Lord Jesus, apart from whom they can do nothing.

Chapter 14—The Works Which Are Counted Good before God

We confess and acknowledge that God has given to man his holy law, in which not only all such works as displease and offend his godly majesty are forbidden, but also those which please him and which he has promised to reward are commanded. These works are of two kinds. The one is done to the honor of God, the other to the profit of our neighbor, and both have the revealed Word of God as their assurance. To have one God, to worship and honor him, to call upon him in all our troubles, to reverence his holy Name, to hear his Word and to believe it, and to share in his holy sacraments, belong to the first kind. To honor father, mother, princes, rulers, and superior powers; to love them, to support them, to obey their orders if they are not contrary to the commands of God, to save the lives of the innocent, to repress tyranny, to defend the oppressed, to keep our bodies clean and holy, to live in soberness and temperance, to deal justly with all men in word and deed, and, finally, to repress any desire to harm our neighbor, are the good works of the second kind, and these are most pleasing and acceptable to God as he has commanded them himself. Acts to the contrary are sins, which always displease him and provoke him to anger, such as, not to call upon him alone when we have need, not to hear his Word with reverence, but to condemn and despise it, to have or worship idols, to maintain and defend idolatry, lightly to esteem the reverend name of God, to profane, abuse, or condemn the sacraments of Christ Jesus, to disobey or resist any whom God has placed in authority, so long as they do not exceed the bounds of their office, to murder, or to consent thereto, to bear hatred, or to let innocent blood be shed if we can prevent it. In conclusion, we confess and affirm that the breach of any other commandment of the first or second kind is sin, by which God's anger and displeasure are kindled against the proud, unthankful world. So that we affirm good works to be those alone which are done in faith and at the command of God who, in his law, has set forth the things that please him. We affirm that evil works are not only those expressly done against God's command, but also, in religious matters and the worship of God, those things which have no other warrant than the invention and opinion of man. From the beginning God has rejected such, as we learn from the words of the prophet Isaiah and of our master, Christ Jesus, "In vain do they worship Me, teaching the doctrines and commandments of men."

Chapter 15—The Perfection of the Law and the Imperfection of Man

We confess and acknowledge that the law of God is most just, equal, holy, and perfect, commanding those things which, when perfectly done, can give life and bring man to eternal felicity; but our nature is so corrupt, weak, and imperfect, that we are never able perfectly to fulfill the works of the law. Even after we are reborn, if we say that we have no sin, we deceive ourselves and the truth of God is not in us. It is therefore essential for us to lay hold on Christ Jesus, in his righteousness and his atonement, since he is the end and consummation of the law and since it is by him that we are set at liberty so that the curse of God may not fall upon us, even though we do not fulfill the law in all points. For as God the Father beholds us in the body of his Son Christ Jesus, he accepts our imperfect obedience as if it were perfect, and covers our works, which are defiled with many stains, with the righteousness of his

Son. We do not mean that we are so set at liberty that we owe no obedience to the law—for we have already acknowledged its place—but we affirm that no man on earth, with the sole exception of Christ Jesus, has given, gives, or shall give in action that obedience to the law which the law requires. When we have done all things we must fall down and unfeignedly confess that we are unprofitable servants. Therefore, whoever boasts of the merits of his own works or puts his trust in works of supererogation, boasts of what does not exist, and puts his trust in damnable idolatry.

Chapter 16—The Kirk

As we believe in one God, Father, Son, and Holy Ghost, so we firmly believe that from the beginning there has been, now is, and to the end of the world shall be, one Kirk, that is to say, one company and multitude of men chosen by God, who rightly worship and embrace him by true faith in Jesus Christ, who is the only Head of the Kirk, even as it is the body and spouse of Christ Jesus. This Kirk is catholic, that is, universal, because it contains the chosen of all ages, of all realms, nations, and tongues, be they of the Jews or be they of the Gentiles, who have communion and society with God the Father, and with his Son, Christ Jesus, through the sanctification of his Holy Spirit. It is therefore called the communion, not of profane persons, but of saints, who, as citizens of the heavenly Jerusalem, have the fruit of inestimable benefits, one God, one Lord Jesus, one faith, and one baptism. Out of this Kirk there is neither life nor eternal felicity. Therefore we utterly abhor the blasphemy of those who hold that men who live according to equity and justice shall be saved, no matter what religion they profess. For since there is neither life nor salvation without Christ Jesus; so shall none have part therein but those whom the Father has given unto his Son Christ Jesus, and those who in time come to him, avow his doctrine, and believe in him. (We include the children with the believing parents.) This Kirk is invisible, known only to God, who alone knows whom he has chosen, and includes both the chosen who are departed, the Kirk triumphant, those who yet live and fight against sin and Satan, and those who shall live hereafter.

Chapter 17—The Immortality of Souls

The chosen departed are in peace, and rest from their labors; not that they sleep and are lost in oblivion as some fanatics hold, for they are delivered from all fear and torment, and all the temptations to which we and all God's chosen are subject in this life, and because of which we are called the Kirk militant. On the other hand, the reprobate and unfaithful departed have anguish, torment, and pain which cannot be expressed. Neither the one nor the other is in such sleep that they feel no joy or torment, as is testified by Christ's parable in St. Luke XVI, his words to the thief, and the words of the souls crying under the altar, "O Lord, thou that art righteous and just, how long shalt thou not revenge our blood upon those that dwell in the earth?"

Chapter 18—The Notes by Which the True Kirk Shall Be Determined from the False, and Who Shall Be Judge of Doctrine

Since Satan has labored from the beginning to adorn his pestilent synagogue with the title of the Kirk of God, and has incited cruel murderers to persecute, trouble, and molest the true Kirk and its members, as Cain did to Abel, Ishmael to Isaac, Esau to Jacob, and the whole priesthood of the Jews to Christ Jesus himself and his apostles after him. So it is essential that the true Kirk be distinguished from the filthy synagogues by clear and perfect notes lest we, being deceived, receive and embrace, to our own condemnation, the one for the other. The notes, signs, and assured tokens whereby the spotless bride of Christ is known from the horrible harlot, the false Kirk, we state, are neither antiquity, usurped title, lineal succession, appointed place, nor the numbers of men approving an error. For Cain was before Abel and Seth in age and title; Jerusalem had precedence above all other parts of the earth, for in it were priests lineally descended from Aaron, and greater numbers followed the scribes, Pharisees, and priests, than unfeignedly believed and followed Christ Jesus and his doctrine; and yet no man of judgment, we suppose, will hold that any of the forenamed were the Kirk of God. The notes of the true Kirk, therefore, we believe, confess, and avow to be: first, the true preaching of the Word of God, in which God has revealed himself to us, as the writings of the prophets and apostles declare; secondly, the right administration of the sacraments of Christ Jesus, with which must be associated the Word and promise of God to seal and confirm them in our hearts; and lastly, ecclesiastical discipline uprightly ministered, as God's Word prescribes, whereby vice is repressed and virtue nourished. Then wherever these notes are seen and continue for any time, be the number complete or not, there, beyond any doubt, is the true Kirk of Christ, who, according to his promise, is in its midst. This is not that universal Kirk of which we have spoken before, but particular Kirks, such as were in Corinth, Galatia, Ephesus, and other places where the ministry was planted by Paul and which he himself called Kirks of God. Such Kirks, we the inhabitants of the realm of Scotland confessing Christ Jesus, do claim to have in our cities, towns, and reformed districts because of the doctrine taught in our Kirks, contained in the written Word of God, that is, the Old and New Testaments, in those books which were originally reckoned as canonical. We affirm that in these all things necessary to be believed for the salvation of man are sufficiently expressed. The interpretation of Scripture, we confess, does not belong to any private or public person, nor yet to any Kirk for pre-eminence or precedence, personal or local, which it has above others, but pertains to the Spirit of God by whom the Scriptures were written. When controversy arises about the right understanding of any passage or sentence of Scripture, or for the reformation of any abuse within the Kirk of God, we ought not so much to ask what men have said or done before us, as what the Holy Ghost uniformly speaks within the body of the Scriptures and what Christ Jesus himself did and commanded. For it is agreed by all that the Spirit of God, who is the Spirit of unity, cannot contradict himself. So if the interpretation or opinion of any theologian, Kirk, or council, is contrary to the plain Word of God written in any other passage of the Scripture, it is most certain that this is not the true understanding and meaning of the Holy Ghost, although councils, realms, and nations have approved and received it. We dare not receive or admit any interpretation which is contrary to any principal point of our faith, or to any other plain text of Scripture, or to the rule of love.

Chapter 19—The Authority of the Scriptures
As we believe and confess the Scriptures of God sufficient to instruct and make perfect the man of God, so do we affirm and avow their authority to be from God, and not to depend on men or angels. We affirm, therefore, that those who say the Scriptures have no other authority save that which they have received from the Kirk are blasphemous against God and injurious to the true Kirk, which always hears and obeys the voice of her own Spouse and Pastor, but takes not upon her to be mistress over the same.

Chapter 20—General Councils, Their Power, Authority, and the Cause of Their Summoning
As we do not rashly condemn what good men, assembled together in general councils lawfully gathered, have set before

us; so we do not receive uncritically whatever has been declared to men under the name of the general councils, for it is plain that, being human, some of them have manifestly erred, and that in matters of great weight and importance. So far then as the council confirms its decrees by the plain Word of God, so far do we reverence and embrace them. But if men, under the name of a council, pretend to forge for us new articles of faith, or to make decisions contrary to the Word of God, then we must utterly deny them as the doctrine of devils, drawing our souls from the voice of the one God to follow the doctrines and teachings of men. The reason why the general councils met was not to make any permanent law which God had not made before, nor yet to form new articles for our belief, nor to give the Word of God authority; much less to make that to be his Word, or even the true interpretation of it, which was not expressed previously by his holy will in his Word; but the reason for councils, at least of those that deserve that name, was partly to refute heresies, and to give public confession of their faith to the generations following, which they did by the authority of God's written Word, and not by any opinion or prerogative that they could not err by reason of their numbers. This, we judge, was the primary reason for general councils. The second was that good policy and order should be constituted and observed in the Kirk where, as in the house of God, it becomes all things to be done decently and in order. Not that we think any policy of order of ceremonies can be appointed for all ages, times, and places; for as ceremonies which men have devised are but temporal, so they may, and ought to be, changed, when they foster superstition rather than edify the Kirk.

Chapter 21—The Sacraments

As the fathers under the law, besides the reality of the sacrifices, had two chief sacraments, that is, circumcision and the passover, and those who rejected these were not reckoned among God's people; so do we acknowledge and confess that now in the time of the gospel we have two chief sacraments, which alone were instituted by the Lord Jesus and commanded to be used by all who will be counted members of his body, that is, Baptism and the Supper or Table of the Lord Jesus, also called the Communion of His Body and Blood. These sacraments, both of the Old Testament and of the New, were instituted by God not only to make a visible distinction between his people and those who were without the Covenant, but also to exercise the faith of his children and, by participation of these sacraments, to seal in their hearts the assurance of his promise, and of that most blessed conjunction, union, and society, which the chosen have with their Head, Christ Jesus. And so we utterly condemn the vanity of those who affirm the sacraments to be nothing else than naked and bare signs. No, we assuredly believe that by Baptism we are engrafted into Christ Jesus, to be made partakers of his righteousness, by which our sins are covered and remitted, and also that in the Supper rightly used, Christ Jesus is so joined with us that he becomes the very nourishment and food for our souls. Not that we imagine any transubstantiation of bread into Christ's body, and of wine into his natural blood, as the Romanists have perniciously taught and wrongly believed; but this union and conjunction which we have with the body and blood of Christ Jesus in the right use of the sacraments is wrought by means of the Holy Ghost, who by true faith carries us above all things that are visible, carnal, and earthly, and makes us feed upon the body and blood of Christ Jesus, once broken and shed for us but now in heaven, and appearing for us in the presence of his Father. Notwithstanding the distance between his glorified body in heaven and mortal men on earth, yet we must assuredly believe that the bread which we break is the communion of Christ's body and the cup which we bless the communion of his blood. Thus we confess and believe without doubt that the faithful, in the right use of the Lord's Table, do so eat the body and drink the blood of the Lord Jesus that he remains in them and they in him; they are so made flesh of his flesh and bone of his bone that as the eternal Godhood has given to the flesh of Christ Jesus, which by nature was corruptible and mortal, life and immortality, so the eating and drinking of the flesh and blood of Christ Jesus does the like for us. We grant that this is neither given to us merely at the time nor by the power and virtue of the sacrament alone, but we affirm that the faithful, in the right use of the Lord's Table, have such union with Christ Jesus as the natural man cannot apprehend. Further we affirm that although the faithful, hindered by negligence and human weakness, do not profit as much as they ought in the actual moment of the Supper, yet afterwards it shall bring forth fruit, being living seed sown in good ground; for the Holy Spirit, who can never be separated from the right institution of the Lord Jesus, will not deprive the faithful of the fruit of that mystical action. Yet all this, we say again, comes of that true faith which apprehends Christ Jesus, who alone makes the sacrament effective in us. Therefore, if anyone slanders us by saying that we affirm or believe the sacraments to be symbols and nothing more, they are libelous and speak against the plain facts. On the other hand we readily admit that we make a distinction between Christ Jesus in his eternal substance and the elements of the sacramental signs. So we neither worship the elements, in place of that which they signify, nor yet do we despise them or undervalue them, but we use them with great reverence, examining ourselves diligently before we participate, since we are assured by the mouth of the apostle that "whoever shall eat this bread, and drink this cup of the Lord, unworthily, shall be guilty of the body and blood of the Lord."

Chapter 22—The Right Administration of the Sacraments

Two things are necessary for the right administration of the sacraments. The first is that they should be ministered by lawful ministers, and we declare that these are men appointed to preach the Word, unto whom God has given the power to preach the gospel, and who are lawfully called by some Kirk. The second is that they should be ministered in the elements and manner which God has appointed. Otherwise they cease to be the sacraments of Christ Jesus. This is why we abandon the teaching of the Roman Church and withdraw from its sacraments; firstly, because their ministers are not true ministers of Christ Jesus (indeed they even allow women, whom the Holy Ghost will not permit to preach in the congregation, to baptize) and, secondly, because they have so adulterated both the sacraments with their own additions that no part of Christ's original act remains in its original simplicity. The addition of oil, salt, spittle, and such like in baptism, are merely human additions. To adore or venerate the sacrament, to carry it through streets and towns in procession, or to reserve it in a special case, is not the proper use of Christ's sacrament but an abuse of it. Christ Jesus said, "Take ye, eat ye," and "Do this in remembrance of Me." By these words and commands he sanctified bread and wine to be the sacrament of his holy body and blood, so that the one should be eaten and that all should drink of the other, and not that they should be reserved for worship or honored as God, as the Romanists do. Further, in withdrawing one part of the sacrament—the blessed cup—from the people, they have committed sacrilege. Moreover, if the sacraments are to be rightly used it is essential that the end and purpose of their institution should be understood, not only by the minister but also by the recipients. For if the recipient does not understand what is being done, the sacrament is not being rightly used, as is seen in the case of the Old Testament sacrifices. Similarly, if the teacher teaches false doctrine which is hateful to God, even though the sacraments are his own ordinance, they are not rightly used, since wicked men have used them for another end than what God had commanded. We affirm that this has been done to the sacraments in the Roman Church, for there the whole action of the Lord Jesus is adulterated in form, purpose, and meaning. What Christ Jesus did, and commanded to be done, is evident from the Gospels and from St. Paul; what the priest does at the altar we do not need to tell. The end and purpose of Christ's institution, for which it should be used, is set forth in the words, "Do this in remembrance of Me," and "For as often as ye eat this bread and drink this cup ye do show"—that is, extol, preach, magnify, and praise—"the Lord's death, till He come." But let the words of the mass, and their own doctors and teachings witness, what is the purpose and meaning of the mass; it is that, as mediators between Christ and his Kirk, they should offer to God the Father, a sacrifice in propitiation for the sins of the living and of the dead. This doctrine is blasphemous to Christ Jesus and would deprive his unique sacrifice, once offered on the cross for the cleansing of all who are to be sanctified, of its sufficiency; so we detest and renounce it.

Chapter 23—To Whom Sacraments Appertain

We hold that baptism applies as much to the children of the faithful as to those who are of age and discretion, and so we condemn the error of the Anabaptists, who deny that children should be baptized before they have faith and understanding. But we hold that the Supper of the Lord is only for those who are of the household of faith and can try and examine themselves both in their faith and their duty to their neighbors. Those who eat and drink at that holy table without faith, or without peace and goodwill to their brethren, eat unworthily. This is the reason why ministers in our Kirk make public and individual examination of those who are to be admitted to the table of the Lord Jesus.

Chapter 24—The Civil Magistrate

We confess and acknowledge that empires, kingdoms, dominions, and cities are appointed and ordained by God; the powers and authorities in them, emperors in empires, kings in their realms, dukes and princes in their dominions, and magistrates in cities, are ordained by God's holy ordinance for the manifestation of his own glory and for the good and well being of all men. We hold that any men who conspire to rebel or to overturn the civil powers, as duly established, are not merely enemies to humanity but rebels against God's will. Further, we confess and acknowledge that such persons as are set in authority are to be loved, honored, feared, and held in the highest respect, because they are the lieutenants of God, and in their councils God himself doth sit and judge. They are the judges and princes to whom God has given the sword for the praise and defense of good men and the punishment of all open evil doers. Moreover, we state the preservation and purification of religion is particularly the duty of kings, princes, rulers, and magistrates. They are not only appointed for civil government but also to maintain true religion and to suppress all idolatry and superstition. This may be seen in David, Jehoshaphat, Hezekiah, Josiah, and others highly commended for their zeal in that cause.

Therefore we confess and avow that those who resist the supreme powers, so long as they are acting in their own spheres, are resisting God's ordinance and cannot be held guiltless. We further state that so long as princes and rulers vigilantly fulfill their office, anyone who denies them aid, counsel, or service, denies it to God, who by his lieutenant craves it of them.

Chapter 25—The Gifts Freely Given to the Kirk

Although the Word of God truly preached, the sacraments rightly ministered, and discipline executed according to the Word of God, are certain and infallible signs of the true Kirk, we do not mean that every individual person in that company is a chosen member of Christ Jesus. We acknowledge and confess that many weeds and tares are sown among the corn and grow in great abundance in its midst, and that the reprobate may be found in the fellowship of the chosen and may take an outward part with them in the benefits of the Word and sacraments. But since they only confess God for a time with their mouths but not with their hearts, they lapse, and do not continue to the end. Therefore they do not share the fruits of Christ's death, resurrection, and ascension. But such as unfeignedly believe with the heart and boldly confess the Lord Jesus with their mouths shall certainly receive his gifts. Firstly, in this life, they shall receive remission of sins and that by faith in Christ's blood alone; for though sin shall remain and continually abide in our mortal bodies, yet it shall not be counted against us, but be pardoned, and covered with Christ's righteousness. Secondly, in the general judgment, there shall be given to every man and woman resurrection of the flesh. The sea shall give up her dead, and the earth those who are buried within her. Yea, the Eternal, our God, shall stretch out his hand on the dust, and the dead shall arise incorruptible, and in the very substance of the self-same flesh which every man now bears, to receive according to their works, glory or punishment. Such as now delight in vanity, cruelty, filthiness, superstition, or idolatry, shall be condemned to the fire unquenchable, in which those who now serve the devil in all abominations shall be tormented forever, both in body and in spirit. But such as continue in well doing to the end, boldly confessing the Lord Jesus, shall receive glory, honor, and immortality, we constantly believe, to reign forever in life everlasting with Christ Jesus, to whose glorified body all his chosen shall be made like, when he shall appear again in judgment and shall render up the Kingdom to God his Father, who then shall be and ever shall remain, all in all things, God blessed forever. To whom, with the Son and the Holy Ghost, be all honor and glory, now and ever. Amen.

Arise, O Lord, and let thine enemies be confounded; let them flee from thy presence that hate thy godly Name. Give thy servants strength to speak thy Word with boldness, and let all nations cleave to the true knowledge of thee. Amen.

NOTES

Preface

1. Roland H. Bainton, *The Reformation of the Sixteenth Century* (Boston: Beacon, 1952), 181.
2. Mark Galli, "The Hard-to-Like Knox," *Christian History* (Issue 46, Vol. XIV, no. 2, 1995), 6.
3. Alexander Smellie, *The Reformation in Its Literature* (London: Andrew Melrose, 1925), 245.
4. Theodore Beza, *Life of John Calvin* (London: L. B. Seeley and Sons, 1834), 76.
5. Patrick Fraser Tytler, *The History of Scotland: From the Accession of Alexander III to the Union* (Edinburgh: William P. Nimmo, 1869), 2:355.
6. John Howie, *The Scots Worthies* (1870; repr., Edinburgh: Banner of Truth, 1995), 52.
7. Ibid., 56–57.
8. Wayne Martindale and Jerry Root, eds., *The Quotable Lewis* (Wheaton, Ill.: Tyndale, 1989), 365.
9. Bainton, *The Reformation of the Sixteenth Century,* 180.
10. Iain Murray, *John Knox: The Annual Lecture of the Evangelical Library for 1972* (London: Evangelical Library; Edinburgh: Banner of Truth, 1973), 3.
11. Howie, *The Scots Worthies*, 63.
12. John Knox, *John Knox's History of the Reformation in Scotland*, William Croft Dickinson, ed. (New York: Philosophical Library, 1950), 1:83.
13. John Knox, cited in Burk Parsons, preface to *John Calvin: A Heart for Devotion, Doctrine, and Doxology*, Burk Parsons, ed. (Lake Mary, Fla.: Reformation Trust, 2008), xv.
14. Thomas Smeaton, cited in Howie, *The Scots Worthies,* 64.

Chapter 1

1. Knox, cited in Murray, *John Knox*, 4.
2. Howie, *The Scots Worthies*, 64.
3. William Croft Dickinson, introduction to Knox, *John Knox's History of the Reformation in Scotland*, 1:xxxi.
4. Ibid., 1:xxxii.
5. J. H. Merle d'Aubigne, *The Reformation in England* (1853; repr., Edinburgh: Banner of Truth, 1994), 1:68.
6. Knox, *John Knox's History of the Reformation in Scotland*, 1:69.
7. Howie, *The Scots Worthies*, 63.
8. Murray, *John Knox*, 7.

9. Will Durant, *The Reformation* (New York: Simon and Schuster, 1957), 607.

10. Bainton, *The Reformation of the Sixteenth Century*, 180.

11. Eustace Percy, *John Knox* (London: James Clarke, 1964), 42.

12. Ibid., 32.

13. Tytler, *The History of Scotland*, 2:21.

14. Percy, *John Knox*, 33.

15. Ibid., 37.

16. Ibid.

17. George Wishart, cited in Knox, *John Knox's History of the Reformation in Scotland*, 1:69.

18. Percy, *John Knox*, 42.

19. Wishart, cited in Knox, *John Knox's History of the Reformation in Scotland*, 2:245.

20. Ibid., 1:74.

21. Cited in ibid., 1:86.

22. Cited in ibid., 1:77–78.

23. Knox, cited in ibid., 1:79.

24. Tytler, *The History of Scotland*, 2:50.

25. Cited in Knox, *John Knox's History of the Reformation in Scotland*, 1:83.

26. Ibid., 1:84–85.

27. Knox, cited in Murray, *John Knox*, 4.

28. Knox, *John Knox's History of the Reformation in Scotland*, 1:95.

29. Ibid., 1:95–97.

30. Thomas McCrie, *Life of John Knox, The Scottish Reformer* (Philadelphia: William S. Marten, 1839), 40.

31. Murray, *John Knox*, 20–21.

32. Cited in Knox, *John Knox's History of the Reformation in Scotland*, 1:108.

33. Ibid., 1:109.

34. Knox, *John Knox's History of the Reformation in Scotland*, 1:111.

35. Merle d'Aubigne, *The Reformation in England*, 1:227.

36. Durant, *The Reformation*, 610.

37. Hugh Latimer, cited in Merle d'Aubigne, *The Reformation in England*, 1:233.

38. Howie, *The Scots Worthies*, 49.

39. Wishart, cited in Percy, *John Knox*, 54.

40. Knox, *John Knox's History of the Reformation in Scotland*, 1:114.

41. Percy, *John Knox*, 133.

42. Merle d'Aubigne, *The Reformation in England*, 1:196.

43. Knox, cited in Murray, *John Knox*, 8.

44. Knox, *John Knox's History of the Reformation in Scotland*, 1:117.

45. Ibid., 1:118.

46. Murray, *John Knox*, 10.

47. George P. Fisher, *The Reformation* (New York: Charles Scribner's Sons, 1912), 302.

48. Howie, *The Scots Worthies*, 50.

49. John Calvin, *Letters of John Calvin* (Edinburgh: Banner of Truth, 1980), 174.

50. Howie, *The Scots Worthies*, 63.

51. Knox, cited in D. G. Hart, "The Reformer of Faith and Life," in Parsons, *John Calvin*, 50.

52. Knox, cited in Murray, *John Knox*, 10.

53. Durant, *The Reformation*, 609.

54. Howie, *The Scots Worthies*, 50–51.

55. Knox, cited in ibid., 52.

56. Durant, *The Reformation*, 609.

57. Fisher, *The Reformation*, 303.

58. Knox, cited in Howie, *The Scots Worthies*, 54.

59. Murray, *John Knox*, 13.

60. Ibid.

61. Knox, cited in ibid.

62. Calvin, *Letters of John Calvin*, 214.

63. J. H. S. Burleigh, *A Church History of Scotland* (London: Oxford University Press, 1973), 149.

64. Scots Confession, Chapter 3 (see Appendix B).

65. Burleigh, *A Church History of Scotland*, 150.

66. Diarmaid MacCulloch, *The Reformation* (New York: Penguin Group, 2003), 292.

67. Smellie, *The Reformation in Its Literature*, 250.

68. Calvin, cited in John Knox, *The Reformation in Scotland* (Edinburgh: Banner of Truth, 1982), 96.

69. Knox, *John Knox's History of the Reformation in Scotland,* 1:92.

70. Knox, cited in Fisher, *The Reformation*, 308.

71. Tytler, *The History of Scotland*, 2:355.

72. Knox, cited in Murray, *John Knox*, 22.

73. Knox, cited in Percy, *John Knox,* 130.

74. Knox, cited in Tytler, *The History of Scotland*, 2:356.

75. Knox, cited in ibid.

76. Ibid.

77. The earl of Morton, cited in ibid.

78. Smeaton, cited in ibid.

Chapter 2

1. Knox, cited in Murray, *John Knox*, 22.

2. Ibid.

3. Knox, cited in McCrie, *Life of John Knox*, 73.

4. Murray, *John Knox*, 22.

5. Burleigh, *A Church History of Scotland*, 154.

6. Ibid.

7. Cited in Dickinson, introduction to Knox, *John Knox's History of the Reformation in Scotland,* 1:lxxxii.

8. Ibid.

9. Knox, cited in David Otis Fuller, *A Treasury of Evangelical Writings* (Grand Rapids: Kregel, 1961), 170.

10. Knox, cited in ibid., 171.

11. Knox, cited in ibid.

12. Knox, *John Knox's History of the Reformation in Scotland,* 1:285.

13. Knox, cited in Durant, *The Reformation,* 608.

14. Knox, cited in Murray, *John Knox,* 5.

15. Knox, cited in Fuller, *A Treasury of Evangelical Writings,* 166.

16. Knox, cited in Calvin, *Letters of John Calvin,* 214.

17. Knox, cited in Fuller, *A Treasury of Evangelical Writings,* 166.

18. Knox, cited in Murray, *John Knox,* 17.

19. Smellie, *The Reformation in Its Literature,* 255.

20. From the hymn "Guide Me, O Thou Great Jehovah" by William Williams, 1745.

Chapter 3

1. Charles H. Spurgeon, cited in Merle d'Aubigne, *The Reformation in England,* 1:18.

2. Knox, cited in Murray, *John Knox,* 4.

3. Howie, *The Scots Worthies,* 57.

4. Knox, cited in Smellie, *The Reformation in Its Literature,* 255.

5. Knox, cited in ibid., 254.

6. Spurgeon, cited in Merle d'Aubigne, *The Reformation in England,* 1:18.

7. John Calvin, *Institutes of the Christian Religion,* ed. John T. McNeill, trans. Ford Lewis Battles (Philadelphia: Westminster, 1960), 3.20.1.

8. Ibid.

9. Ibid., 3.20.3.

10. Ibid., 3.20.21.

11. Ibid.

12. Knox, cited in Henry Cowan, *John Knox: The Hero of the Scottish Reformation* (London: G. P. Putnam's Sons, 1905), 336.

13. Knox, cited in Calvin, *Letters of John Calvin,* 214.

14. Ibid., 238.

15. Ibid.

16. Mary Guise, cited in Howie, *The Scots Worthies,* 57.

17. Percy, *John Knox,* 52.

18. John Knox, *A Treatise on Prayer, or, a Confession, and Declaration of Prayers,* cited in *Selected Writings of John Knox: Public Epistles, Treatises, and Expositions to the Year*

1559 (Dallas: Presbyterian Heritage Publications, 1995). Viewed online at http://www.swrb.com/newslett/actualNLs/prayertr.htm, 1.

19. Ibid., 7.
20. Ibid., 6.
21. Knox, cited in McCrie, *Life of John Knox*, 72.
22. Knox, *John Knox's History of the Reformation in Scotland*, 1:lxxxiv.
23. Knox, cited in Tytler, *The History of Scotland*, 2:356.
24. Howie, *The Scots Worthies*, 123.
25. Ibid., 124.
26. Ibid., 138.

Chapter 4

1. Knox, cited in Fuller, *A Treasury of Evangelical Writings*, 172.
2. Dickinson, introduction to Knox, *John Knox's History of the Reformation in Scotland*, 1:xv.
3. Cited in ibid., 1:xix.
4. Cited in ibid., 1:xxii.
5. Percy, *John Knox*, 53.
6. Knox, cited in Fuller, *A Treasury of Evangelical Writings*, 172.
7. Knox, cited in Murray, *John Knox*, 21.
8. Lewis, cited in Martindale and Root, *The Quotable Lewis*, 365.
9. Knox, cited in Murray, *John Knox*, 4.
10. Knox, cited in Smellie, *The Reformation in Its Literature*, 248.
11. Knox, cited in Tytler, *The History of Scotland*, 356.
12. Knox, cited in Murray, *John Knox*, 21.
13. James Melville, cited in Fisher, *The Reformation*, 323.
14. Knox, cited in Percy, *John Knox*, 53.
15. Murray, *John Knox*, 17.
16. Knox, cited in ibid., 18.
17. Knox, cited in Durant, *The Reformation*, 608.
18. Knox, cited in Percy, *John Knox*, 130.
19. Durant, *The Reformation*, 610.
20. Knox, cited in Smellie, *The Reformation in Its Literature*, 247.
21. Knox, cited in Murray, *John Knox*, 22.
22. Knox, cited in ibid., 10.
23. Burleigh, *A Church History of Scotland*, 157.
24. Smellie, *The Reformation in Its Literature*, 246.
25. Knox, cited in ibid.
26. Knox, cited in Percy, *John Knox*, 53.
27. Knox, cited in Murray, *John Knox*, 17.

28. Knox, cited in Fuller, *A Treasury of Evangelical Writings*, 165.

29. Calvin, *Institutes of the Christian Religion*, 3.16.1.

30. Knox, *John Knox's History of the Reformation in Scotland*, 1:93.

31. Ian Hamilton, expounding Psalm 88, April 21, 2010.

32. Smellie, *The Reformation in Its Literature*, 240.

33. Patrick Hamilton, cited in ibid., 238.

34. Knox, cited in Fuller, *A Treasury of Evangelical Writings*, 169.

35. Scots Confession, chap. 13 (see Appendix B).

36. Ibid.

37. Ibid., chap. 16.

38. Knox, *John Knox's History of the Reformation in Scotland*, 1:84.

39. Ibid., 1:85.

40. Ibid., 1:86.

41. Burleigh, *A Church History of Scotland*, 143.

42. Percy, *John Knox*, 240.

43. Cited in Dickinson, introduction to Knox, *John Knox's History of the Reformation in Scotland*, 1:xlvii.

44. Ibid., 1:xlii.

45. Knox, cited in Sydney Smith, *The Edinburgh Review: or Critical Journal*, Vols. 134–135 (July 1871): 53.

46. Burleigh, *A Church History of Scotland*, 144.

47. Murray, *John Knox*, 21.

48. Knox, cited in Howie, *The Scots Worthies*, 55.

49. Knox, cited in Fisher, *The Reformation*, 308.

50. Bainton, *The Reformation of the Sixteenth Century*, 181.

Chapter 5

1. Percy, *John Knox*, 51.

2. Knox, cited in Durant, *The Reformation*, 610.

3. Percy, *John Knox*, 52.

4. Ibid., 51.

5. Knox, *John Knox's History of the Reformation in Scotland*, 1:284.

6. Knox, cited in Percy, *John Knox*, 217–218.

7. Ibid., 216.

8. Calvin, cited in ibid.

9. Knox, cited in Durant, *The Reformation*, 612.

10. Knox, *John Knox's History of the Reformation in Scotland*, 1:118.

11. Ibid., 1:285.

12. Knox, cited in Durant, *The Reformation*, 611.

13. Smellie, *The Reformation in Its Literature*, 265.

14. C. S. Lewis, cited in Martindale and Root, *The Quotable Lewis*, 365.

15. Durant, *The Reformation*, 611.
16. John Knox, *Two Comfortable Epistles to His Afflicted Brethren in England (1554)*, Kevin Reed, ed. (Dallas: Presbyterian Heritage Publications, 1995). http://www.swrb.com/newslett/actualnls/TwoEpist.htm. Accessed June 22, 2010.
17. Ibid.
18. Ibid.
19. Burleigh, *A Church History of Scotland*, 156.
20. Knox, cited in McCrie, *Life of John Knox*, 9.
21. Burleigh, *A Church History of Scotland*, 150.
22. Knox, *John Knox's History of the Reformation in Scotland*, 1:284.
23. Smellie, *The Reformation in Its Literature*, 264.
24. Thomas Carlyle, cited in ibid., 265.

Chapter 6

1. John Knox, *The Works of John Knox*, David Laing, ed. (Edinburgh: Johnstone and Hunter, 1856), V:25–26.
2. Martindale and Root, *The Quotable Lewis*, 365. Lewis here is citing the popular view of Knox.
3. Murray, *John Knox*, 3.
4. Knox, *The Works of John Knox*, V:24.
5. Jonathan Edwards, *Basic Writings* (New York: New American Library, 1966), 83.
6. As part of a committee interviewing a church-planting candidate, I asked how Reformed soteriology would affect his approach to planting a church. He replied: "You mean Calvinism? I don't have any problem with it." His check-the-box assent puzzled me. I wonder how we would respond if he had said: "You mean justification by faith alone? I don't have any problem with it."
7. Calvin, *Letters of John Calvin*, 250.
8. Edwards, *Basic Writings*, 83.
9. Scots Confession, chap. 16.
10. Scots Confession, chap. 7.
11. Smellie, *The Reformation in Its Literature*, 247.
12. James S. McEwen, *The Faith of John Knox* (London: Lutterworth, 1961), 69.
13. Knox, *The Works of John Knox*, V:25–26.
14. Ibid., V:26.
15. Ibid., V:25–26.

Chapter 7

1. Knox, cited in Smellie, *The Reformation in Its Literature*, 254.
2. Knox, cited in G. R. Elton, *Renaissance and Reformation: 1300–1648* (New York: Macmillan, 1963), 179.
3. Knox, *Two Comfortable Epistles to His Afflicted Brethren in England (1554)*. http://www.swrb.com/newslett/actualnls/TwoEpist.htm. Accessed June 24, 2010.

4. Knox, cited in Smellie, *The Reformation in Its Literature*, 254.

5. Knox, cited in Dickinson, introduction to Knox, *John Knox's History of the Reformation in Scotland*, 1:lxxxiv.

6. Ibid., 1:lxxxiii.

7. Knox, cited in ibid.

8. Geddes MacGregor, *The Thundering Scot* (Philadelphia: Westminster, 1957), 229–31.

9. Knox, cited in Smellie, *The Reformation in Its Literature*, 265.

10. Knox, cited in ibid., 248.

11. Knox, *John Knox's History of the Reformation in Scotland*, 2:276.

12. Knox, cited in Tytler, *The History of Scotland*, 2:356.

13. Kenneth Scott Latourette, *A History of Christianity* (Peabody, Mass.: Prince Press, 1975), 2:772.

14. Durant, *The Reformation*, 610.

15. Knox, *John Knox's History of the Reformation in Scotland*, 1:114.

16. Neil Postman, *The Disappearance of Childhood* (New York: Vintage, 1994), 39.

17. Knox, cited in Smellie, *The Reformation in Its Literature*, 251.

18. Burleigh, *A Church History of Scotland*, 173.

19. Ibid., 160.

20. Bainton, *The Reformation of the Sixteenth Century*, 182.

21. Latourette, *A History of Christianity*, 2:771.

22. Smellie, *The Reformation in Its Literature*, 264.

Chapter 8

1. Thomas Carlyle, *On Heroes and Hero-Worship and the Heroic in History* (London: J. M. Dent & Sons, 1924), 381.

2. Howie, *The Scots Worthies*, 63.

3. Ibid.

4. Galli, *The Hard-to-Like Knox*, 6.

5. James Anthony Froude, cited in Howie, *The Scots Worthies*, 64.

6. Ibid., 65.

7. Ibid.

8. Bainton, *The Reformation of the Sixteenth Century*, 182.

9. Tytler, *The History of Scotland*, 2:318.

10. Knox, cited in Howie, *The Scots Worthies*, 62–63.

11. Knox, cited in Tytler, *The History of Scotland*, 2:356.

12. Carlyle, *On Heroes and Hero-Worship and the Heroic in History*, 381.

13. Knox, cited in Howie, *The Scots Worthies*, 61.

14. Ibid., 63.

15. Knox, *John Knox's History of the Reformation in Scotland*, 1:284.

16. Knox, cited in Parsons, *John Calvin: A Heart for Devotion, Doctrine, and Doxology*, xv.

BIBLIOGRAPHY

Bainton, Roland H. *The Reformation of the Sixteenth Century.* Boston: Beacon, 1952.

Beza, Theodore. *Life of John Calvin.* London: L. B. Seeley and Sons, 1834.

Burleigh, J. H. S. *A Church History of Scotland.* London: Oxford University Press, 1973.

Calvin, John. *Institutes of the Christian Religion.* John T. McNeill, ed. Ford Lewis Battles, trans. Philadelphia: Westminster, 1960.

_____. *Letters of John Calvin.* Edinburgh: Banner of Truth, 1980.

Carlyle, Thomas. *On Heroes and Hero-Worship and the Heroic in History.* London: J. M. Dent and Sons, 1924.

Cowan, Henry. *John Knox: The Hero of the Scottish Reformation.* London: G. P. Putnam's Sons, 1905.

Durant, Will. *The Reformation.* New York: Simon and Schuster, 1957.

Edwards, Jonathan. *Basic Writings.* New York: New American Library, 1966.

Elton, G. R. *Renaissance and Reformation: 1300–1648.* New York: Macmillan, 1963.

Fisher, George P. *The Reformation.* New York: Charles Scribner's Sons, 1912.

Fuller, David Otis. *A Treasury of Evangelical Writings.* Grand Rapids: Kregel, 1961.

Galli, Mark. "The Hard-to-Like Knox." *Christian History.* Issue 46, Vol. XIV, no. 2, 1995.

Howie, John. *The Scots Worthies.* 1870; repr., Edinburgh: Banner of Truth, 1995.

Knox, John. *John Knox's History of the Reformation in Scotland.* William Croft Dickinson, ed. New York: Philosophical Library, 1950.

_____. *Selected Writings of John Knox: Public Epistles, Treatises, and Expositions to the Year 1559.* Dallas: Presbyterian Heritage Publications, 1995.

_____. *Two Comfortable Epistles to His Afflicted Brethren in England (1554)*. Kevin Reed, ed. Dallas: Presbyterian Heritage Publications, 1995.

_____. *The Works of John Knox*. David Laing, ed. Edinburgh: Johnstone and Hunter, 1856.

Latourette, Kenneth Scott. *A History of Christianity*. Peabody, Mass.: Prince Press, 1975.

MacCulloch, Diarmaid. *The Reformation*. New York: Penguin Group, 2003.

MacGregor, Geddes. *The Thundering Scot*. Philadelphia: Westminster, 1957.

Martindale, Wayne, and Jerry Root, eds. *The Quotable Lewis*. Wheaton, Ill.: Tyndale, 1989.

McCrie, Thomas. *Life of John Knox, The Scottish Reformer*. Philadelphia: William S. Marten, 1839.

McEwen, James S. *The Faith of John Knox*. London: Lutterworth, 1961.

Merle d'Aubigne, J. H. *The Reformation in England*. 1853; repr., Edinburgh: Banner of Truth, 1994.

Murray, Iain. *John Knox: The Annual Lecture of the Evangelical Library for 1972*. London: Evangelical Library; Edinburgh: Banner of Truth, 1973.

Parsons, Burk, ed. *John Calvin: A Heart for Devotion, Doctrine, and Doxology*. Lake Mary, Fla.: Reformation Trust, 2008.

Percy, Eustace. *John Knox*. London: James Clarke, 1964.

Postman, Neil. *The Disappearance of Childhood*. New York: Vintage, 1994.

Smellie, Alexander. *The Reformation in Its Literature*. London: Andrew Melrose, 1925.

Tytler, Patrick Fraser. *The History of Scotland: From the Accession of Alexander III to the Union*. Edinburgh: William P. Nimmo, 1869.

INDEX

ABOUT THE AUTHOR

Douglas Bond is the head of the English Department at Covenant High School in Tacoma, Wash., where he teaches literature, writing, and history. He also lectures on literature and church history, and leads frequent historical study tours in Europe.

He holds a graduate degree in English education from St. Martin's University and a preliminary certificate in theology from Moore Theological College in Australia. He is an ordained ruling elder in the Presbyterian Church in America.

Bond has written numerous works of fiction, many of them for young people, including the *Crown & Covenant* trilogy (focusing on a Covenanter family in Scotland) and the *Faith & Freedom* trilogy (following the same family to Revolutionary America). His fictional works also include a novel about John Calvin, *The Betrayal.* Among his nonfiction titles are *Stand Fast in the Way of Truth* and *Hold Fast in a Broken World.*

Bond and his wife, Cheryl, have four sons and two daughters. They live in Tacoma.

To learn more, visit his web site, www.bondbooks.net.